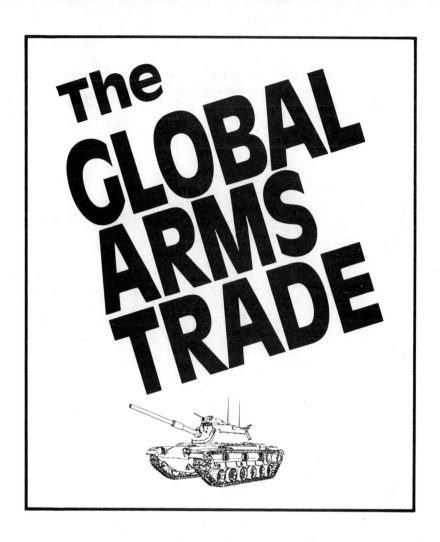

The GLOBAL ARMS TRADE

Gary E. McCuen

IDEAS IN CONFLICT SERIES

502 Second Street
Hudson, Wisconsin 54016
Phone (715) 386-7113

Illustrations & Photo Credits

Center for Defense Information 40, 61 Ollie Harrington 21, 67 Office of Technology Assessment 25, 55, 106, 120 Ron Swanson 50, 72, 93 U.S. Air Force 99 U.S. Arms Control and Disarmament Agency 32, 80, 86 U.S. Department of Defense 11, 114. Cover illustration by Ron Swanson.

© 1992 by Gary E. McCuen Publications, Inc.
502 Second Street, Hudson, Wisconsin 54016

(715) 386-7113

International Standard Book Number
0-86596-082-8 Printed in the United States of America

CONTENTS

Ideas in Conflict   6

CHAPTER 4 CURBING WORLD ARMS SALES: IDEAS IN CONFLICT

REASONING SKILL DEVELOPMENT

These activities may be used as individualized study guides for students in libraries and resource centers as discussion catalysts in small group and classroom discussions.

IDEAS in CONFLICT ®

This series features ideas in conflict on political, social, and moral issues. It presents counterpoints, debates, opinions, commentary, and analysis for use in libraries and classrooms. Each title in the series uses one or more of the following basic elements:

Introductions *that present an issue overview giving historic background and/or a description of the controversy.*

Counterpoints *and debates carefully chosen from publications, books, and position papers on the political right and left to help librarians and teachers respond to requests that treatment of public issues be fair and balanced.*

Symposiums *and forums that go beyond debates that can polarize and oversimplify. These present commentary from across the political spectrum that reflect how complex issues attract many shades of opinion.*

A *global* *emphasis with foreign perspectives and surveys on various moral questions and political issues that will help readers to place subject matter in a less culture-bound and ethnocentric frame of reference. In an ever-shrinking and interdependent world, understanding and cooperation are essential. Many issues are global in nature and can be effectively dealt with only by common efforts and international understanding.*

Reasoning skill *study guides and discussion activities provide ready-made tools for helping with critical reading and evaluation of content. The guides and activities deal with one or more of the following:*

RECOGNIZING AUTHOR'S POINT OF VIEW

INTERPRETING EDITORIAL CARTOONS

VALUES IN CONFLICT

WHAT IS EDITORIAL BIAS?

WHAT IS SEX BIAS?

WHAT IS POLITICAL BIAS?

WHAT IS ETHNOCENTRIC BIAS?

WHAT IS RACE BIAS?

WHAT IS RELIGIOUS BIAS?

*From across **the political spectrum** varied sources are presented for research projects and classroom discussions. Diverse opinions in the series come from magazines, newspapers, syndicated columnists, books, political speeches, foreign nations, and position papers by corporations and nonprofit institutions.*

About the Editor

Gary E. McCuen is an editor and publisher of anthologies for public libraries and curriculum materials for schools. Over the past years his publications have specialized in social, moral and political conflict. They include books, pamphlets, cassettes, tabloids, filmstrips and simulation games, many of them designed from his curriculums during 11 years of teaching junior and senior high school social studies. At present he is the editor and publisher of the *Ideas in Conflict* series and the *Editorial Forum* series.

CHAPTER 1

INTRODUCTION

INTRODUCTION

THE GLOBAL ARMS TRADE: PAST AND PRESENT

Geoffrey Kemp

Geoffrey Kemp is Senior Associate of the Carnegie Endowment for International Peace. This reading consists of material from a project on "Arms Control and the Proliferation of High Technology Weapons in the Near East and South Asia." The project was funded by grants from the Mac-Arthur Foundation and the U.S. Institute of Peace.

Points to Consider:

1. Describe, in your own words, the three elements of the current global arms race that are most disturbing to the author.

2. Who are the biggest sellers of arms around the world? What are they selling? Give several specific examples.

3. Why has missile technology become so important in the global arms trade?

4. Why does the U.S. continue to supply arms to the Middle East and South Asia? What are the Soviet goals in arms sales in this region?

Excerpted from testimony submitted by Geoffrey Kemp before the House Committee on Foreign Affairs, May 17, 1990.

The superpowers can slow down the regional arms race but they can't stop or reverse it.

The improvement in U.S.-Soviet relations and the anticipation of major cuts in NATO and Warsaw Pact forces has led to speculation that the two superpowers may now cooperate to diffuse regional arms races, especially those in the Near East and South Asia (NESA) region. How likely is this to happen and will the regional countries take kindly to such overtures?

The outlook is cloudy at best. There is consensus that the NESA arms race is particularly scary; the dangers of the spread of weapons of mass destruction and their delivery systems in the NESA region have received much attention in the past two months.

History of Proliferation

Faced with these multiple challenges, what should the priorities of regional diplomacy be and who is to decide these priorities? Is it practical to tackle the arms problem in the absence of on-going negotiations to end the most important conflicts: Arab-Israel, Iran-Iraq, and India-Pakistan? Should arms control efforts be focused on multilateral approaches or are there specific steps the superpowers can take independently? Some of these questions arise from the new circumstances of U.S.-Soviet cooperation. But the problem is by no means new, and there is a long history of squabbling over the role of arms transfers in this region and efforts to exert some control over the process.

The Balkan countries before World War I were fertile ground for competitive arms sales by the major European powers. It was German military and financial assistance to Turkey that helped contain the allied offensive in the Dardanelles and keep Turkey in the war on the side of the Central powers. Later in the war, it was British military assistance to King Faisal, who, with the help of Colonel Lawrence, launched the Arab revolt against Turkish occupation, and played a crucial role in weakening the resistance of the Ottoman empire.

After World War II, arms supplies from both legal and illegal sources to the newly founded State of Israel played a central role in Israel's victory during the 1948-49 War of Independence. During the early 1950s, Britain, France, and the United States imposed an arms rationing scheme on Israel and the Arabs administered by the Near East Arms Coordinating Committee (NEACC). It was effective until France broke ranks and supplied

The Boeing E-3 Airborne Warning and Command
System (AWACS), currently the most advanced early
warning system of its kind, is one of several procurement
projects that may be affected by current debates in Japan
over the future of defense collaboration
with the United States.

Israel with advanced aircraft and the Soviet Union entered the region by concluding massive arms deals with Syria and Egypt in 1955.

During the 1950s, Britain and the United States were the major arms suppliers to, respectively, India and Pakistan. When China and India went to war in 1962, the United States rushed military assistance to India's beleaguered forces. But three years later, when war between India and Pakistan broke out, both Britain and the United States embargoed arms supplies to the sub-continent. As a result, China and the Soviet Union became major suppliers to, respectively, Pakistan and India. During the 1970s, the combination of rising oil prices and Britain's decision to leave the Persian Gulf resulted in a massive infusion of Western arms to both Iran and the oil-rich Arabs. And when the Soviet Union invaded Afghanistan in 1980, the United States once more became the predominant arms supplier to Pakistan.

Even the present hullabaloo over missile proliferation and efforts to bring it under control has at least a thirty year history. In the 1950s Egypt—then the United Arab Republic—began a serious ballistic missile development program and recruited West German engineers to lead the design effort. President Kennedy

---

ARMED TO THE HILT

In 1990, Egypt, India, Iraq, Israel, and Syria will have had more main battle tanks in their inventories than either Britain or France, the former colonial powers. Israel and Iraq has more armored personnel carriers, and India has more combat aircraft than any other NATO country with the exception of the United States.

Geoffrey Kemp, excerpted from hearings before the Committee on Foreign Affairs, May 17 and July 11, 1990

---

sent his coordinator for disarmament activities, John J. McCloy, on a mission to Egypt and Israel in June 1963 to try to obtain assurances that Egypt "would not acquire sophisticated weapons such as West German 'ground-to-ground missiles'" and that Israel would not "initiate 'cross-border military action' nor develop nuclear weapons." McCloy's arguments to President Nasser about the dangers of proliferation convinced the latter that missiles, indeed, had great political importance. McCloy came home empty-handed and never went to Israel.

The Current Arms Race

Despite this colorful backdrop of history, there are at least three elements of the present arms race which are new and disturbing. First, the quantity and quality of arms in the NESA region have reached unprecedented levels, and the ability of regional military forces to project power far beyond their borders has increased. Second, the Iran-Iraq war demonstrated the effectiveness, under certain conditions, of chemical weapons and surface-to-surface missiles and has raised fears about the further spread of weapons of mass destruction, including nuclear weapons. Third, new suppliers—the so-called Second Tier—have entered the arms market and can provide some of the weapons which were previously the monopoly of the superpowers and the Europeans.

The regional powers spend most of their defense budgets on modern conventional weapons, not the more publicized surface-to-surface missiles and weapons of mass destruction. The numbers are impressive. In 1990, Egypt, India, Iraq, Israel, and Syria all had more main battle tanks in their inventories than either Britain or France, the former colonial powers. Israel and

Iraq has more armored personnel carriers, and India has more combat aircraft than any other NATO country with the exception of the United States. India has the world's third largest army and the seventh largest navy. Syria and Egypt have forces far larger than Spain.

Numbers alone provide a broad brush view of the arms race but in terms of the quality of the weapons, the picture is equally striking. The array of "conventional" equipment includes top of the line American items such as the Abrams main battle tank (Egypt and Saudi Arabia), F-15 fighters (Saudi Arabia and Israel), F-16 fighters (Egypt, Israel and Pakistan), Improved-Hawk surface-to-air missiles (Kuwait, Saudi Arabia and Israel). The best Soviet equipment has also been transferred to the NESA region, including Mig-29s (India, Syria and Iraq) and SU-24s (Libya), and a Soviet nuclear submarine which was received "on loan" by India.

Britain, France and China have also sold their best fighter aircraft to Saudi Arabia, Iraq and Pakistan. Britain concluded two agreements with Saudi Arabia in February 1986 and 1988, the Al-Yamanah I and II, which included the sale of 118 Tornado fighter jets, 48 Hawk light fighters, 90 Black Hawk helicopters, and a number of trainer aircraft. These two agreements, worth $10 billion and $20 billion respectively, represent the largest aircraft sale ever between the United Kingdom and a NESA country. France has supplied its nuclear-capable state-of-the-art Mirage 2000 fighter aircraft to both Egypt and India. China has supplied a large number of fighter aircraft to Pakistan and Egypt, among other countries in the region.

India, Israel and, to a lesser extent, Iran, Syria, Libya, Egypt and Saudi Arabia now have conventional military forces that can operate at increasing distances from their borders, posing potential threats to a wider number of neighbors. India's growing power projection capabilities have been recently demonstrated with interventions in Sri Lanka and the Maldives and are indicative of India's determination to become a major Indian Ocean power.

Chemical Weapons

The technological lack of sophistication of chemical weapons has made them an attractive alternative to nuclear weapons for Third World nations trying to acquire weapons of mass destruction. Long banned from the stage of international armed conflict, the use of chemical weapons in the Iran-Iraq conflict has once again raised the specter of their possible widespread

13

MAJOR RECIPIENTS OF U.S. AND SOVIET ARMS TRANSFERS 1984-1988*

U.S.	U.S.S.R.
Israel	Iraq
Saudi Arabia	India
Japan	Vietnam`
Australia	Cuba
Taiwan	Syria
Egypt	Afghanistan
South Korea	Angola
Spain	Ethiopia
Pakistan	Libya
Thailand	North Korea

*Excludes NATO and Warsaw Pact countries

Table prepared by Center for Defense Information

use in future conflicts. While their military effectiveness should not be exaggerated, they did demonstrate their utility both as tactical battlefield weapons and as a means to instill terror among the civilian population. First documented in March 1983, Iraq used chemicals against soldiers and later, its own Kurdish population.

Libya, Syria, and Iran, as well as Egypt and Israel, are believed to have active chemical weapons programs. Before the Persian Gulf War, Iraq was reported to have maintained the largest chemical weapons program in the NESA region. Iraq was believed to have been producing mustard gas, at the Samarra facility, 70 km northwest of Baghdad, and nerve agents, including the deadly nerve agents sarin and tabun. Iraq is also believed to have had a research and development center at Salman Pak which was also used for biological weapons research.

Iran's chemical weapons industry, which was developed to acquire a retaliatory capability against Iraqi CW attacks, has its main production plant in the vicinity of Tehran, and produces mustard gas, blood agents, and nerve agents. The Syrians reportedly have expanded their program in the last five years with the aid of technology from Western European corporations.

They maintain a large research center near Damascus and are believed to have developed a chemical warhead for their Scud-B missiles. Finally, Libya was believed to be in possession of the largest chemical weapons production plant in the Third World, until a fire apparently damaged part of the facility on March 14, 1990.

Missile Technology

Surface-to-surface ballistic missiles (SSM) with widely varying ranges, payload, and accuracies have been deployed in Algeria, Egypt, Iraq, Iran, Israel, Kuwait, Libya, North Yemen, South Yemen, Saudi Arabia, and Syria. Most of these missiles are obsolescent, Soviet-designed unguided rockets, Frogs, and first generation guided missiles, SCUDs, which have limited range and poor accuracy and are not deployed in large numbers. Though most of these systems are far from state-of-the-art missile technology, countries in the NESA region have been very successful at modifying and enhancing their capabilities. Iraq has been particularly successful at this endeavor. Faced with the lack of a retaliatory capability when Iran began to launch missile attacks on Baghdad, Iraq embarked upon an ambitious project to extend the range of its Soviet-supplied SCUD-B missiles. By means of reducing the warhead compartment and thus leaving more room for the missile propellent, Iraq developed the 600-700 km range Al-Hussayn missile and the 900 km Al-Abbas. (During the Gulf War, SCUD missile attacks reached Israel and Saudi Arabia.)

Israel also has an impressive missile arsenal, with the U.S.-supplied short-range Lance and the indigenously developed Jericho I and II. At the same time Israel continues to push full speed ahead with the Shavit, its satellite launching vehicle which on April 2, 1990, placed the 160 Kg Ofeq-2, Israel's second satellite, in orbit. Depending on the estimates, an Israeli missile based on the Shavit could have a range of 5200 to 7200 km, both sufficient to hit Moscow and all targets within the Middle East.

Syria possesses a small number of more accurate but short-range Soviet SS-21s, and is reported to be actively trying to purchase Chinese-made 600 km range M-9 missiles, currently under development, after the Soviet Union refused to sell Syria the longer-range SS-23 missiles, which are slated for destruction as a result of the INF treaty with the United States.

India and Pakistan both have short-range missile programs under development. On September 27, 1989, India test-fired a

250 km range single-stage, liquid-fueled, short-ranged missile named Prithvi. The Prithvi, which can carry a payload of 1000 kilograms and is nuclear-capable, is reported to be almost ready for delivery to the Indian Army and Air Force.

Nuclear Weapons

Concerning nuclear weapons there is now overwhelming evidence that Israel is a fully-fledged nuclear weapons power and that India and Pakistan have nuclear weapons production capabilities. The recent sale by France of a nuclear reactor to Pakistan has further increased the speculation that Pakistan is actively pursuing a nuclear weapons program. In 1990, a sting operation arranged by U.S. and British officials led to the arrest of a number of Iraqi citizens who were attempting to smuggle nuclear detonators called krytrons out of Heathrow airport. Iraq described the issue as an attempt by Western media to discredit Iraq and give Israel an excuse to launch a strike against Iraq's nuclear and military installations.

Rumors have begun circulating again that Iran is gearing up its nuclear program, with one report stating that Iran is seeking a nuclear fuel production capability.

The spread of chemical and nuclear weapons is now entering a decisive phase. Fully-fledged nuclear weapons programs in Israel, India, Pakistan, Iran, North Korea, South Africa, Brazil, and Argentina could develop in the next ten years. The establishment of networks within the existing and potential nuclear powers of the Third World is making it easier to circumvent traditional nuclear control mechanisms. Reports of a South African-Israeli nuclear connection are paralleled by reports of a link between China and Pakistan.

New Suppliers

A third reason for concern is the changing relationships among the supplier countries and the impact this will have on efforts to implement arms control regimes. In the past, U.S.-Soviet rivalry provided a bonus for many NESA countries who were able to obtain large quantities of military grant assistance or low interest loans by playing one side off against the other.

However, while the draw-down of competitive aid programs will mean less assistance, it does not mean the superpowers will opt out of the arms market. Each superpower retains strategic interests in the region and each has a large arms industry seeking profitable ventures with regional countries who can pay their way. Furthermore, it is this market that keeps Britain and France actively involved and has attracted new suppliers, including China, Argentina, North Korea, South Korea, and Brazil. China has emerged as an important arms supplier, providing a wide selection of basic weapons including combat aircraft, tanks, missiles, artillery, submarines and small arms. During the mid-1980s, when the Iran-Iraq war was at its peak, China was the largest arms exporter in the developing world. Although in no way comparable to the United States and USSR in terms of its exporting capacity, China has carved out a corner of the arms market as a supplier of less sophisticated conventional technology sold at cut-rate prices. It should also be remembered that in East Europe and the Soviet Union, there are thousands of skilled weapons specialists who may take advantage of the freedom to travel to work for profit in those regional countries who can pay hard currency. Trying to put a cap on the transfer of people will be much more difficult than controlling technology.

There is also a growing indigenous arms capability in the region, with Israel and India in possession of the most sophisticated industries. Israel has been active in the arms market for many years, and in 1988 it exported a record $1.47 billion in arms to 61 nations. The first half of 1989 saw a 40 percent increase in sales of Israel Aircraft Industries, 75 percent of which was accounted for by increases in exports. India announced it, too, would begin to promote foreign arms sales. Egypt, Iran, and Pakistan have strong production capabilities in certain categories of weapons, especially ammunition and small arms.

Taken together, these three developments suggest that unless arms limitation regimes are soon put in place, the region may well indeed be beyond control. To assess the prospects for arms control, it is first necessary to briefly review U.S. and Soviet regional policy.

U.S. Policy

American policy in the Near East and South Asia is driven by several geopolitical objectives which, to date, have overridden arms control considerations. One objective is to keep the oil-rich resources of the region from falling into hostile hands. This requires good military relations with the key Arab countries. A second objective is the defense and survival of Israel, which means providing military assistance while seeking a diplomatic solution to the Arab-Israeli conflict. A third objective is to retain friendly relations with India and Pakistan, the world's largest and fifth largest democracies respectively.

Soviet Policy

The Soviet Union likewise has to balance its strategic and arms control interests in the region, irrespective of its relations with the United States. These interests derive from its geography and the political turmoil along the Soviet Union's southern border including ethnic violence and intense nationalist sentiment in the Republics of Georgia, Armenia, Azerbaijan, Turkmenistan, Uzbekistan, and Tajikstan, and the continued war in Afghanistan. Whatever type of entity the Soviet Union becomes, it is bound to have important relations with the key Near East countries and Israel and South Asia. It will therefore remain sensitive to direct or indirect military threats emanating from this region. Like the United States, the Soviet Union will probably continue to see it in its interest to sell arms to selected regional countries, both for reasons of influence and economic benefits.

The arms race in this region poses some clear strategic and political problems for the Soviet Union. The countries which will have the most sophisticated military capabilities in the coming decade—India, Israel, and Pakistan—will all be able to target the Soviet Union, rather than the United States. Turkey, Iran and Afghanistan will all have the capacity, at least in theory, to arm dissident groups within the Soviet Union.

Curbing the Arms Trade

While it is very much in the United States' interest to pursue multilateral arms control initiatives, the resistance of the regional powers and the complexities in resolving questions of equity and verification make it unlikely that there will be any significant breakthrough in the near term. Even in the case of the Chemical Weapons Treaty, a way will have to be found to address the Arab arguments about Israel's nuclear weapons.

Therefore, quite aside from what happens with multilateral arms control and the peace process, the United States has strong interests in working more informally with others to defuse several urgent proliferation problems.

At a time when the superpower relationship is changing beyond all expectations, schemes for greater U.S.-Soviet cooperation to diffuse regional conflict, including greater restrictions on weapons transfers, have encouraging possibilities. The superpowers can slow down the regional arms race but they can't stop or reverse it. To do that requires the cooperation of the key regional players and the linking of the arms control agenda to the search for regional conflict resolution.

INTERPRETING EDITORIAL CARTOONS

This activity may be used as an individualized study guide for students in libraries and resource centers or as a discussion catalyst in small group and classroom discussions.

Although cartoons are usually humorous, the main intent of most political cartoonists is not to entertain. Cartoons express serious social comment about important issues. Using graphic and visual arts, the cartoonist expresses opinions and attitudes. By employing an entertaining and often light-hearted visual format, cartoonists may have as much impact on national and world issues as editorial and syndicated columnists.

Points to Consider

1. Examine the cartoon in this activity. (See next page)

2. How would you describe the message of this cartoon? Try to describe the message in one to three sentences.

3. Do you agree with the message expressed in the cartoon? Why or why not?

4. Does this cartoon support the author's point of view in this reading? Why or why not?

"They just started their session, and I guess you
can get ready to welcome them back."

CHAPTER 2

THE GLOBAL MARKETPLACE: AN OVERVIEW

2   THE GLOBAL MARKETPLACE: AN OVERVIEW

GLOBAL DEFENSE BUSINESS AND ARMS PROLIFERATION

Office of Technology Assessment

The following statement was taken from an Office of Technology report on the global arms trade and the manufacture and sale of weapons. This report was requested by the Senate Committee on Armed Services and the House Committee on Government Operations.

Points to Consider:

1. How have many nations learned to produce arms?

2. Where do poor nations of the world get their arms?

3. How strong financially is the U.S. arms industry?

4. Why does the arms trade make the world a more dangerous place?

5. What different policy issues and options are discussed?

Office of Technology Assessment, "The Global Arms Trade: Commerce in Advanced Military Technology and Weapons," Washington, D.C., June, 1991.

International arms business, in which the United States is first among several prominent suppliers, is building up a dangerously armed world.

The war in the Persian Gulf graphically demonstrated the consequences of extensive international commerce in powerful advanced conventional weapons. At the same time, the end of the Cold War and the accompanying decline in defense spending have weakened the political foundation for continuing arms transfers and enhanced the economic motivations for international arms sales. Worldwide, the defense industries face deep recession (and probable permanent adjustment to much lower levels of production) brought on by a general erosion of demand and continued strong overcapacity of production.

Technology Transfer

The proliferation of the ability to produce modern arms (emanating principally from the United States and Europe) has led directly and indirectly to the arming of our adversaries as well as our friends. As OTA (Office of Technology Assessment) previously reported, U.S. companies played a major role in the transfer of sophisticated defense technology to Europe, Japan, and elsewhere. This was accomplished largely through international industrial collaboration, including joint ventures, licensed production, codevelopment, and direct offsets.

The United States and Europe routinely transfer a great deal of advanced defense technology to less developed nations. In 1988, for example, India, Egypt, Indonesia, South Korea, Taiwan, and Brazil were producing 43 different major weapons under international licensing agreements. As a consequence, several of these nations have attained significant defense industrial capacity and have entered the arms export business. Between 1978 and 1988, the arms exported by Israel, Brazil, Spain, and South Korea amounted to $16 billion. The multiplicity of sources (both advanced and developed countries) has produced a buyer's market in which a range of modern defense equipment is generally available to any nation that can pay for it.

Financial Trouble

A final factor influencing policy is that many U.S. defense companies are in financial trouble. Decreased procurement budgets and the rapidly escalating cost of weapons systems have combined to threaten the long-term economic viability of

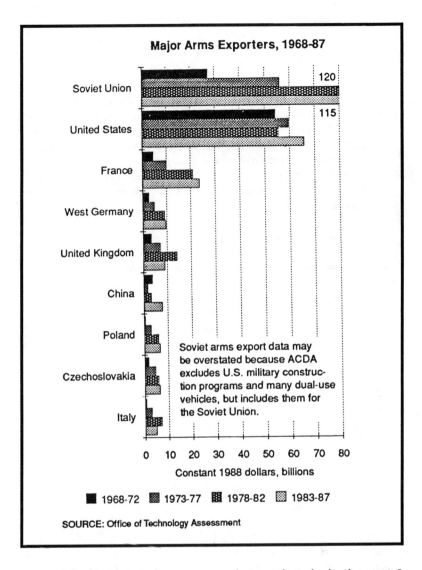

Major Arms Exporters, 1968-87

Soviet Union — 120

United States — 115

France

West Germany

United Kingdom

China

Poland

Czechoslovakia

Italy

Soviet arms export data may be overstated because ACDA excludes U.S. military construction programs and many dual-use vehicles, but includes them for the Soviet Union.

0 10 20 30 40 50 60 70 80

Constant 1988 dollars, billions

■ 1968-72   ▨ 1973-77   ▩ 1978-82   ▦ 1983-87

SOURCE: Office of Technology Assessment

many defense companies as presently constituted. In the past 3 years, a handful of U.S. firms have collectively written off over $3.5 billion in R&D (Research and Development) investments. The impact of decreased defense business—large lay-offs and production cut-backs—has been and will continue to be felt in congressional districts across the nation.

Some defense executives would like to expand international sales and collaborative ventures to increase their customer base and revenues in a declining market. But they have been hindered by government ambivalence, by rapidly increasing foreign competition, and by limited demand in many markets. International business has been important to a number of major U.S. defense producers for many years; it will be increasingly critical to some companies as U.S. military procurement budgets continue to fall in the 1990s. Some important weapons plants may have to shut down, and defense executives argue that international sales could keep them open. These factors generate strong pressures for international collaboration in defense technology and for export of top-of-the-line military equipment.

Foreign Military Sales

The United States has never viewed arms transfers primarily as a sector in international trade. Indeed, a substantial amount of equipment and training is transferred through various grant programs. In addition, the Foreign Military Sales (FMS) program is structured to place foreign policy goals above economic considerations. In an FMS sale, the recipient country makes a formal request to the United States for security assistance, the State Department evaluates the request from a policy standpoint (and may or may not authorize it), and the Department of Defense implements it. In most cases, the U.S. Government then buys the equipment from U.S. companies and transfers it at cost (plus a 3 percent administrative fee) to the recipient nation.

In recent years, however, direct commercial sales (DCS), in which a U.S. company delivers arms directly to a foreign corporation or government, have expanded significantly. In a direct sale, a U.S. company and a foreign government (or firm) reach an agreement and then apply for the requisite permissions and export licenses. Compared to an FMS sale, profits from DCS sales are often higher, accountability to the U.S. government is less, and the overall relevance to U.S. foreign policy goals is usually smaller and less direct.

A Dangerous World

International arms business, in which the United States is first among several prominent suppliers, is building up a dangerously armed world. In the Middle East, arms imported to the region have raised the stakes associated with political instability and have figured prominently in the calculations of militant religious regimes and regional strongmen. As the Islamic revolution in Iran has shown, once transferred, modern weapons can outlast the governments they were intended to support. As the war with Iraq has shown, arms may outlast the good will of the leaders to whom they were supplied.

If the goal is to stem proliferation of advanced conventional weapons and defense technology, multilateral restraint by Europe, the Soviet Union, and the United States is a prerequisite. Because these three account for about 80 percent of all arms exports, an agreement to restrain exports could have far-reaching implications. In the context of a "new world order," conventional arms control is clearly an alternative to a continuing arms bazaar, especially in the Middle East. Without the stimulus of a polarizing U.S.-Soviet military confrontation, continued proliferation of arms to the Third World has lost much of its military and political justification. Considering its recent role in the Persian Gulf crisis, the United Nations may be the appropriate vehicle to pursue multilateral restraint of defense exports.

The Policy Dilemma

The state of the international defense business links two issues of current concern to Congress: controlling the proliferation of modern weapons and defense technology and the health of U.S. defense companies. It is likely that a strong consensus could be forged on either issue in isolation, but because of the linkage, the steps needed to implement a solution to one would tend to undermine resolving the other.

Efforts to control proliferation will almost certainly limit the international sales of U.S. defense companies. Similarly, efforts by U.S. defense companies to expand their international operations will exacerbate the problem of proliferation.

There is general agreement that uncontrolled proliferation of advanced weapons is not in the overall interest of the United States. No one wants regional instability or potent military threats to U.S. interests abroad. But there is less agreement on how much proliferation is too much, where proliferation is dangerous, and to what extent arms transfers can be used effectively as tools of foreign influence.

Historical Perspective

Congress has rarely intervened aggressively in the U.S. foreign military sales program. As a result, the executive branch has exercised considerable latitude in the definition and conduct of arms sales and the transfer of defense technology. This is evident from the extreme change of policy from the Carter to the Reagan Administrations. President Jimmy Carter saw the transfer of arms "as an exceptional foreign policy implement, to be used only in instances where it can be clearly demonstrated that the transfer contributes to promote our security and the security of our close friends. Four years later, President Reagan took the other extreme approach. Arms transfers would be "an essential element of [U.S.] global defense posture and an indispensable component of its foreign policy."

Although the President has recently proposed that major supplier nations exercise "collective self restraint" in arms sales to the Middle East, the Bush Administration has also taken the following steps to support foreign sales of U.S. defense equipment. It had previously directed U.S. embassy personnel to increase the level of assistance provided to U.S. defense companies, created the Center for Defense Trade within the State Department, and proposed an arrangement that would allow free and open trade in arms and defense technology within the NATO Alliance, and with other U.S. allies. In March 1991, the Administration proposed that the Export-Import Bank guarantee up to $1 billion in commercial loans to members of NATO, Australia, Japan, and Israel to purchase defense equipment from U.S. contractors.

Recent press reports indicate that the U.S. Army and Air Force are for the first time publicly supporting exports of weapons such as the M1A1 Abrams tank and the F-16 Falcon fighter to keep domestic plants running. Prior to May 1991, the Bush Administration had also used weapons transfers liberally in support of its Persian Gulf policies. It proposed the sale of over $26 billion in U.S. weapons to a variety of countries in the

Middle East. In his address to a joint session of Congress following the end of the Persian Gulf War, the President pressed Congress for greater latitude in arms transfers.

There is, then, a continuing tension not only between Congress and the Executive concerning arms transfers, but also between the policy of arming our allies and the desire to prohibit the export of advanced weapons and technology to potentially hostile or irresponsible nations. The recent Persian Gulf experience will most likely increase these tensions.

Transferring Defense Technology to Developing Nations

The developing nations depend far more heavily on transferred defense technology than do Japan and the Western European states.

Increasingly, U.S. industry transfers defense technology to a wide range of developing nations on an ad hoc basis in the absence of consistent policy direction. Congress faces a clear policy choice: whether or not (or to what extent) to permit U.S. companies to build up the defense production capabilities of the developing world. The principal considerations on which policy in this area might be based are discussed below.

The Future of Global Arms Trade

Frequently objections are offered to any U.S. policy to place additional restraints on international defense trade. Some defense industrialists contend that international sales are important to sustain selected sectors of the U.S. defense industries at present levels of production and capacity. Most industry analysts agree that U.S. Government procurement will continue to fall, and that foreign markets, especially in the Middle East and the Western Pacific, offer opportunities for growth. Proponents urge government to support or, at a minimum, permit expanded foreign sales to cushion the effect of declining domestic procurement.

Many analysts argue, however, that contraction in the defense industries is now appropriate, given significant overcapacity both in the United States and abroad. The expansion of the defense industries in the 1980s apparently cannot be economically sustained into the 1990s. As the potential for hostilities between the United States and the Soviet Union has diminished, large defense budgets have become unnecessary and politically unpopular. In this view, a smaller, more efficient defense industrial base can meet the nation's security needs in the post-Cold War era.

3   THE GLOBAL MARKETPLACE: AN OVERVIEW

ARMS SALES TO THIRD WORLD NATIONS

Richard F. Grimmett

Richard F. Grimmett is a specialist in national defense and Foreign Affairs. The following article is excerpted from his article on arms sales to the Third World nations.

Points to Consider:

1. Why are more attempts being made to sell arms in foreign markets?

2. What has the U.S. government done to promote arms sales abroad?

3. How has the value of arms sales agreements and deliveries to Third World nations changed in recent times?

4. What two nations have sold the most arms to Third World nations between 1983-1990?

5. How did the Iran-Iraq War influence global arms sales?

Richard F. Grimmett, "Conventional Arms Transfers to the Third World, 1983-1990," Congressional Reference Service, August 2, 1991.

For the first time since 1983, the United States ranked first in arms transfer agreements with the Third World.

Because of reductions in defense procurement in the United States resulting from the Cold War's end, American arms producers began to focus greater attention on obtaining foreign markets for their weapons to compensate partially for shrinking domestic orders. By late 1990, U.S. executive branch officials decided to offer government support for American arms exporters and began plans to seek Congressional approval for a $1 billion pilot program. Reductions in domestic defense spending also occurred in major arms supplying nations in Europe, while their traditional foreign arms sales programs continued. Arms exports by European suppliers have generally been much more important to the vitality of their defense industries than has been the case for those of the United States.

The net result of these events has been the development of an intense competition for a greater share of the existing and prospective Third World arms market. Various arms producers in the United States and in foreign countries face the prospect of having to close production lines for certain weapons systems if they cannot secure sufficient export contracts.

The inability or unwillingness of some Third World arms purchasers to pay for their weapons on a timely basis has also reduced their attractiveness as clients. This suggests that in the near future only those Third World nations that clearly have the means to pay for their weapons will be likely to obtain them. This seems certain to make the oil-rich nations of the Near East a continuing focus of major marketing efforts by arms manufacturers of many nations attempting to deal with the economic consequences of the Cold War's end.

In 1991, however, a new element was added to the arms transfer equation: the prospect of an arms transfer restraint policy for the Near East region, and perhaps, ultimately, for the rest of the world. Support for this initiative resulted from concerns stimulated by Iraq's massive arms buildup in the 1980s, which facilitated its invasion and temporary occupation of Kuwait. Should the key arms supplying nations agree to regulate arms transfers to the Near East region—the largest arms market in the Third World—it could result in notable reductions in overall Third World arms trade.

General Trends in Arms Transfers to the Third World

The general decline in the value of new arms transfer

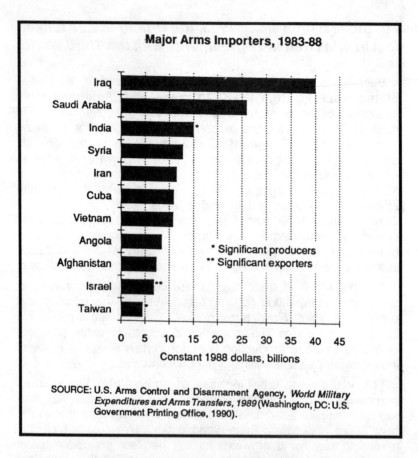

Major Arms Importers, 1983-88

Iraq	
Saudi Arabia	
India	*
Syria	
Iran	
Cuba	
Vietnam	
Angola	
Afghanistan	
Israel	**
Taiwan	*

* Significant producers
** Significant exporters

0   5   10   15   20   25   30   35   40   45
Constant 1988 dollars, billions

SOURCE: U.S. Arms Control and Disarmament Agency, *World Military Expenditures and Arms Transfers, 1989* (Washington, DC: U.S. Government Printing Office, 1990).

agreements with the Third World seen in recent years was reversed in 1990. The value of all arms transfer agreements with the Third World in 1990 was $41.3 billion. This was the first year since 1987 when the total value of arms transfer agreements with the Third World increased over the previous year (in constant 1990 dollars). The end of the Iran-Iraq war in mid-1988 and the scaling back of other regional conflicts such as the civil war in Angola have contributed to a general lack of growth in the Third World arms market since 1987. Were it not for the Kuwait crisis in August 1990 and the major new arms agreements it helped stimulate, it is likely that the figures for total Third World arms transfer agreements for calendar year 1990 would have either remained at roughly 1989 levels or continued their decline.

At the same time, in 1990 the value of all arms deliveries to the Third World ($26.3 billion) was the lowest of any year during the period from 1983-1990. This is the third consecutive year since 1987 that the value of all arms deliveries to the Third World dropped significantly. This pattern reflects the impact of the end of the Iran-Iraq war and the winding down of other regional conflicts in the Third World (in constant 1990 dollars). However, if most arms transfer agreements concluded with the Third World in 1990 are fully implemented, then the total value of arms deliveries may increase in future years.

The Soviet Union and the United States have dominated the Third World arms market as the top two suppliers from 1983-1990. Collectively, the two superpowers accounted for over 60 percent of all arms transfer agreements with and arms deliveries to the Third World during these years.

Many recipient nations in the Third World continue to absorb the weaponry they bought in the late 1970s and early 1980s and are not purchasing large numbers of new, expensive items. In recent years, purchases have included a greater proportion of spare parts, ammunition, and support services, items much less costly than major weapons systems such as combat aircraft, main battle tanks, or ships. The Iraqi invasion of Kuwait in August 1990 did, however, accelerate major purchases by key Persian Gulf states. This reversed the overall pattern of decline in Third World arms transfer agreements that began after 1987.

Many Third World countries continue to be burdened by significant debts and are thus unable or unwilling to commit the funds necessary to obtain additional weapons they might otherwise buy. Some oil-rich nations in the Third World have made more selective purchases in recent years as oil revenues have declined, and they have sought various concessions from suppliers to offset the costs involved in procuring weapons. These factors apply in differing ways to individual countries. But their collective effect throughout the Third World has been to keep the arms market generally flat, with few exceptions.

United States

In 1990, the total value, in real terms, of U.S. arms transfer agreements with the Third World increased dramatically from the pervious year's total, rising from nearly $8 billion in 1989 to $18.5 billion in 1990. For the first time since 1983, the United States ranked first in arms transfer agreements with the Third World. The U.S. share of the value of all such agreements was 44.8 percent in 1990, up from 23.6 percent in 1989 (in constant 1990 dollars).

The extraordinary increase in the value of U.S. arms transfer agreements in 1990 is directly attributable to very costly new orders from Saudi Arabia. In 1990, the value of Saudi Arabia's arms transfer agreements with the United States was over $14.5 billion. These agreements constituted 78.7 percent of all U.S. arms transfer agreements with the United States and also exceeded the total value ($12.1 billion) of all arms transfer agreements made by the Soviet Union with the entire Third World in the same year.

And, as the dramatic events surrounding the Kuwait crisis of 1990 demonstrated, the United States will make major sales of advanced arms to friendly Third World states whenever its government believes that U.S. national interests are served by doing so.

Soviet Union

The total value of the Soviet Union's agreements fell from $13 billion in 1989 to $12.1 billion in 1990. The Soviet Union registered a significant decline in its share of Third World arms transfer agreements, falling from 38.5 percent in 1989 to 29.2 percent in 1990.

During the 1983-1990 period, Soviet arms transfer agreements with the Third World ranged from a low of $8.6 billion to a high of $26.1 billion. But with the exception of 1987, Soviet agreement totals have declined from those of the previous year from 1985 through 1990.

However, the Soviet Union has had long-standing supplier relationships with many of the leading purchasers of weapons in the Third World.

It likely reflects, in part, Soviet cutbacks on costly commitments to some traditional clients that have been involved in regional conflicts that are ending.

China

In the 1980s, China emerged as an important supplier of arms to the Third World, in large measure due to agreements with Iran and Iraq. The value of China's agreements with the Third World reached a peak of nearly $5.2 billion in 1987. China ranked fourth among all suppliers in the value of its arms transfer agreements with the Third World from 1987-1990. In 1990 China ranked third among all suppliers with nearly $2.6 billion in arms transfer agreements (a 6 percent share of all such agreements).

As a nation able and willing to supply a wide variety of basic weapons and ammunition cheaply, and in quantity, China was well positioned to take advantage of the wartime requirements of Iran and Iraq. During the 1983-1990 period, over 48.4 percent of all of China's arms transfer agreements with the Third World were with Iran and Iraq collectively. During the years 1987-1990, China became Iran's largest single arms supplier, concluding agreements valued at over $3 billion and making deliveries valued at nearly $2.4 billion.

It is not clear whether China will be able to sustain its level of arms sales to the Near East region now that the Iran-Iraq war has ended and it is a party to discussions aimed at regulating arms transfers to this region. Of particular interest is China's ability and willingness to sell various missiles throughout the Third World.

Major West European Suppliers

The four major West European suppliers (France, United Kingdom, Germany and Italy) registered a decline in their collective share of all arms transfer agreements with the Third World in 1990, falling to 10.3 percent from 22.4 percent in 1989. Of these suppliers, France suffered a notable decline in the value of its agreements from $3.7 billion in 1989 to $2.2 billion in 1990. The value of the United Kingdom's agreements also fell substantially from $2.7 billion in 1989 to $1.6 billion in 1990. Germany registered a significant decrease in the value of its agreements from $886 million in 1989 to $190 million in 1990. Italy's decrease in agreements value was marginal, falling from $268 million in 1989 to $230 million in 1990 (in constant 1990 dollars).

Throughout the period from 1983-1990, the major West European suppliers, as a group, averaged over 17 percent of all arms transfer agreements with the Third World. Throughout the

35

1983-1990 period, individual suppliers within the major West European group have had exceptional years for arms agreements, such as France in 1984 ($7.9 billion) and 1989 ($3.7 billion), and the United Kingdom in 1985 ($10.4 billion) and 1988 ($5.2 billion) (in constant 1990 dollars). Such totals have generally reflected conclusion of exceptionally large arms transfer agreements with a major Third World purchaser.

Since the four major West European suppliers produce both advanced and basic ground, air, and naval weapons systems, they have the capability to compete successfully with the United States, and in certain instances, with the Soviet Union, for arms sales contracts throughout the Third World. Because these major West European suppliers do not usually tie their arms sales decisions to foreign policy considerations but essentially to economic ones, they have provided a viable alternative source of arms for nations to whom the United States will not sell for policy reasons. Generally strong government marketing support for foreign arms sales enhances the competitiveness of weapons produced by these major West European suppliers.

The Iran-Iraq Arms Market

The trade in arms with Iran and Iraq was a significant element of the entire Third World arms market during the period 1983-1990. The war between these two nations created an urgent demand by both belligerents, throughout most of the 1980s, for conventional weapons of all kinds, from the least sophisticated battlefield consumables to more advanced combat vehicles, missiles and aircraft. During their war, Iran and Iraq bought arms from both major and minor arms suppliers. In the aftermath of the war, some arms-supplying nations continued to maintain a supply relationship with the combatants that had been forged during the war itself. Other suppliers sought to establish a new relationship where possible.

Leading Third World Arms Recipients

Saudi Arabia and Iraq have been, by a wide margin, the top two Third World arms purchasers from 1983-1990, making arms transfer agreements of $57.3 billion and $30.4 billion, respectively, during these years (in current dollars). The total value of all Third World arms transfer agreements from 1983-1990 was $301.7 billion (in current dollars). Thus, Saudi Arabia and Iraq were responsible for 19 percent and 10.1 percent, respectively, of all Third World arms transfer agreements during this time period.

Five of the ten leading Third World arms recipients registered declines in the value of their arms transfer agreements from 1983-1986 to 1987-1990. Some of these declines were significant. All recipients registering major declines were principal customers of the Soviet Union: Iraq declined 51.4 percent, Syria 22.7 percent, India 19 percent and Vietnam 15.2 percent.

Despite large increases in the values of arms transfer agreements by some of the top ten Third World arms recipients, the data reflect only an overall 7 percent increase in new arms transfer agreements by the top ten nations collectively from 1983-1986 to 1987-1990.

Saudi Arabia ranked first among all Third World recipients in the value of arms transfer agreements In 1990, concluding $18.65 billion in such agreements. The United States was its major supplier.

The Soviet Union was the major supplier to five of the top ten recipients of arms transfer agreements in 1990 (Afghanistan, Iran, India, Cuba and Vietnam).

Eight of the top ten Third World arms recipients registered declines in the values of their arms deliveries from 1983-1986 to 1987-1990. Some declines were substantial. Iraq fell 48.5 percent from $26.1 billion to $13.4 billion; Syria fell 38.9 percent, from nearly $8.6 billion to $5.2 billion; Egypt fell 37.8 percent, from $6 billion to $3.7 billion (in current dollars).

The Soviet Union was the major supplier to six of the top ten arms recipients in the Third World in 1990 (Afghanistan, India, Iran, Cuba, Vietnam and Syria).

Saudi Arabia was the leading recipient of arms in the Third World in 1990, receiving over $6.7 billion in deliveries. The United Kingdom was its major supplier.

THE GLOBAL MARKETPLACE: AN OVERVIEW

THE ARMS TRADE AND WORLD HUNGER

George Ayittey

George Ayittey is a visiting Ghanaian Professor of Economics at The American University, Washington, D.C.

Points to Consider:

1. What role did the military play in African history?

2. Who introduced military rule to Africa?

3. How much do African nations spend on military preparations?

4. Who benefits from this military spending?

George Ayittey, "Hungry for Guns," **New Internationalist,** July, 1991.

Three-quarters of the global arms trade involves exports to developing countries.

Amna was grinding millet when it happened. She was six months pregnant. The other women had just come back from their day's work in the sorghum fields and were chattering and laughing. Their laughter faded as they heard the distinctive rumble of army tanks. Within minutes army troops swooped into the town, rounded up a large group of about 400 people — women, men, children — and, accusing them of collaborating with "the enemy", the soldiers drove two tanks over the people, machine-gunning those who tried to escape.

Amna survived because she fell under the trunk of a large tree. Feigning death, she lay until nightfall among the carnage of her fellow townspeople. Five small children, covered by their parents, also survived and wandered screaming among the bodies. Amna heard soldiers arguing about whether to kill the children. Finally they agreed not to waste bullets: the children would soon die of thirst anyway.

Around 80,000 people fled the town of She-eb in northeastern Eritrea that day as the army looted and burned the shops. Soldiers also slaughtered 10,000 sheep, goats, cattle and camels, putting carcasses down the town's only well, thus polluting it forever.

The brutalities were committed by former dictator Colonel Mengistu's Ethiopian army, which was waging civil war against the Eritrean People's Liberation Front. Such events were common in Ethiopia — but by no means limited to that country. Military atrocities are rife in many African nations — like Sudan, Nigeria, Ghana, Uganda, Somalia and Zaire, to name but a few. Civil wars and "final offensive" campaigns give military regimes excuses to perpetrate atrocities against innocent peasants which are reminiscent of Africa's colonial past.

Naive Westerners think true freedom came to Africa after independence from colonial rule. To them a black man governing a black African nation is enough to mean the country has been liberated. They do not distinguish between peasants — the real people of Africa — and their crocodile rulers. Burdened by collective guilt over the iniquities of colonialism, these Westerners shy away from condemning atrocities meted out by "educated" African heads of state against their own people: the slaughter of African peasants. But let a mere 100 African giraffes be killed and the whole Western world would erupt in deafening outrage.

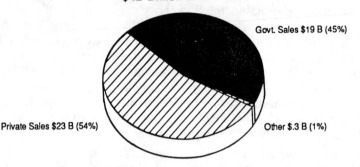

Record U.S. Military Exports
$42 Billion In FY 1991

Govt. Sales $19 B (45%)

Private Sales $23 B (54%)

Other $.3 B (1%)

Government sales: Foreign military sales (FMS) and foreign military construction sales (FMCS). *Private sales:* Sales by companies to foreign governments. *Other:* International Military Education and Training (IMET) and Military Assistance Program (MAP) deliveries.

Sources: DOD, State Dept., CDI, Chart prepared by Center for Defense Information

More infuriating still are the African intellectuals who vehemently defend military rule as uniquely African, based upon African warrior tradition. This is nonsense.

Many ethnic groups did not have standing armies. In the face of imminent external threat, the chief would summon young men of a certain age and present them to the king for war. After a war the army was disbanded so that the military did not drain the economy. In the Yoruba kingdom the *kankafo* — or military head of the war chiefs — was under strict orders never to enter the capital city and thereby stage a coup.

Only in a few African empires and kingdoms such as Dahomey and Zulu did the military play an active role in government. But three or four examples out of over 2,000 chiefdoms, kingdoms and empires in Africa's history hardly constitute "a traditional pattern." Even then, the Dahomean and Zulu military did not turn their guns against their own people. Those pre-colonial soldiers knew their function. Shamefully, modern soldiers in Africa are not so educated in this matter.

EXPANDING MARKETPLACE: MORE SELLERS, MORE BUYERS

	1968	1988
Exporters		
Total Countries	21	45
Third World	1	16
Importers		
Total Countries	74	116
Third World	44	84

Sources: ACDA, CDI

Table prepared by Center for Defense Information

Spending Spree

The modern military is a colonial institution introduced by Europeans into Africa primarily to suppress African liberation struggles. Military rule is as alien and un-African as colonial rule itself—and the military has become the scourge of Africa and the bane of its development. While public services disintegrate, African dictators squander scarce resources on the military.

The proportion of African funds going to equip and pay for armies has been steadily rising—over 40 percent in Ethiopia, 25 percent in Mauritania and 20 percent in Mali. Uganda spends over half of its annual budget on defense. Some of the poorest countries spend more on their military than on health and education.

This pattern is repeated elsewhere in the developing world—with arms spending rocketing from only $1 billion in 1960 to nearly $35 billion in 1987. Three-quarters of the global arms trade involves exports to developing countries.

Who is cashing in on this? The industrialized nations, of course. During the 1980s, NATO countries supplied 31 percent of Third World arms, France 11 percent and the Warsaw Pact countries 58 percent. Instead of stability, these purchases have brought chaos and carnage to the very peasants who sweat and toil to earn Africa the foreign exchange to buy these weapons.

Last year in Sudan, for example, the ruling Moslem North deliberately blocked supplies to the hungry South and even bombed relief sites. Then, unbelievably, the Bashir regime exported 300,000 tons of sorghum—a staple food—to Libya and Iraq in order to buy more arms to use against rebels in the south.

Peasant Anger

As wars rage, food production per head has fallen consistently in Africa over the past 30 years, and Africa's exports have steadily declined, reducing the continent's share of world trade by more than half what it was in 1960.

In the words of Ghanaian peasant Amoafo Yaw:

"The weapons used to butcher the people all come from the farmers' cocoa and coffee money. This has been going on since the days of the colonial masters. . .and our own governments have continued the system. . . .But the farmers have unconsciously decided they will no longer increase cocoa and coffee production and other items which the State depends on for foreign exchange."

But the military fufu-heads can always find the resources to purchase weapons and rain bullets on the people. Even the World Bank, not renowned for its humanitarian policies, is beginning to express concern at the level of military spending by African governments.

And *West Africa* magazine, which historically avoided criticizing African governments, has also begun to complain: ". . .one million dollars could provide 1,000 classrooms for 30,000 children, and yet it is the cost of a modern tank," it points out. "The price of a single helicopter is equivalent to the salary of 12,000 schoolteachers. The policy choice of more tanks means fewer classrooms, with inevitable consequences for economic growth and social development. . . ."

Even some military officers are speaking out and making the links between their countries' economic crisis and soaring military expenditure. For example, former Nigerian Head of State, General Yakubu Gowon, recently came out with this statement:

"The military intervention in politics in 1966 started a chain of reaction whose deleterious effects are still relevant in our national life today. . . .The military should not get itself involved in politics. The sooner they leave the stage the better, or else the people may rise up against them."

Collaboration

Various appeals have been made to industrialized nations to stop the flow of arms to Africa. If Western governments and the International Monetary Fund (IMF) would stop giving loans to dictators in the Third World, they would not be able to terrorize their nations — let alone extend their actions into the international arena.

But do Western governments and the IMF listen? For years they have propped up African regimes that savagely repress their own people — as in countries like Liberia, Kenya and Somalia.

In the words of one Kenyan: "I see the aid that the U.S. is giving President Daniel Arap Moi as a weapon to fight the people of Kenya". Aid, he went on to say, should be tied to human rights and should be given on condition that the country at least observe its own constitution.

When the World Bank and the IMF insisted on making a $70 million loan to the brutal Barre dictatorship in Somalia during 1989, Somali exiles in Washington were outraged. They staged demonstrations outside the grey offices of the IMF and the World Bank.

"It is immoral madness!" exclaimed one furious demonstrator. "How can we be expected to pay back the money and interest on what will at once be side-tracked to subsidize the murder of our mothers and fathers, our brothers and sisters?"

Fooled

It has now become abundantly clear that appeals, exhortations and preaching aren't going to end the slaughter in Africa. Nor are destructive civil wars like those in Ethiopia or Liberia or Sudan.

The West is being fooled — and is colluding in the deceit. It knows of the billions kept in Swiss banks by the kleptocrats. "Every franc we send impoverished Africa comes back to France or is smuggled into Switzerland and even Japan," wrote the Paris daily *Le Monde* in March 1990.

So what can be done? There is, I believe, only one solution. Support for military regimes has to be removed — both inside and outside the country. A military regime does not depend only upon loyal armed forces but also upon the cooperation of civil servants and intellectuals. By going on strike, civil servants may withdraw that support and bring down the regime. It happened twice in Ghana—in 1978 and 1979—and in Benin in 1989.

But removing support from within the country is not enough, as long as rich foreign arms-selling and aid-donating nations continue giving support from the outside.

Perhaps a lesson can be drawn from the experience of Bangladesh, where main opposition parties warned donor countries and agencies that any money loaned during the rule of President Hossain Mohammad Ershad would not be paid back.

The money had been hoarded by Ershad and his cronies, but the people, warned Begum Khaleda Zia, would "not bear the pressure of paying the debt." Aid donors responded by withholding funds and two weeks later the military government of President Ershad collapsed.

So it can be done. The question is when will the industrialized world stop propping up dictators, selling them arms and feeding the militarism that is costing the lives of millions of African peasants?

WHAT IS EDITORIAL BIAS?

This activity may be used as an individualized study guide for students in libraries and resource centers or as a discussion catalyst in small group and classroom discussions.

The capacity to recognize an author's point of view is an essential reading skill. The skill to read with insight and understanding involves the ability to detect different kinds of opinions or bias. **Sex bias, race bias, ethnocentric bias, political bias and religious bias** are five basic kinds of opinions expressed in editorials and all literature that attempts to persuade. They are briefly defined in the glossary below.

Glossary of Terms for Reading Skills

Sex Bias—the expression of dislike for and/or feeling of superiority over the opposite sex or a particular sexual minority

Race Bias—the expression of dislike for and/or feeling of superiority over a racial group

Ethnocentric Bias—the expression of a belief that one's own group, race, religion, culture or nation is superior. Ethnocentric persons judge others by their own standards and values.

Political Bias—the expression of political opinions and attitudes about domestic or foreign affairs

Religious Bias—the expression of a religious belief or attitude

Guidelines

1. From the readings in Chapter Two, locate five sentences that provide examples of editorial opinion or bias.

2. Write down each of the above sentences and determine what kind of bias each sentence represents. Is it **sex bias, race bias, ethnocentric bias, political bias or religious bias?**

45

3. Make up one sentence statements that would be an example of each of the following: **sex bias, race bias, ethnocentric bias, political bias and religious bias.**

4. See if you can locate five sentences that are factual statements from the readings in Chapter Two.

CHAPTER 3

THE MIDDLE EAST ARMS BAZAAR

THE MIDDLE EAST ARMS BAZAAR

IRAN-CONTRA DEALINGS WERE IMMORAL

Penny Lernoux

Penny Lernoux is Latin American Affairs writer for the National Catholic Reporter.

Points to Consider:

1. Why does the author believe that the Iran-Contra Affair was socially immoral?

2. Discuss the issue of "crimes" vs. "mistakes". How does the authors view compare to that of the Congressional opinions in Readings 10 and 11?

3. How must education help to rectify the contradictions of morality in our society?

Penny Lernoux "No One Seemed to Notice Irangate Was Immoral," **National Catholic Reporter,** March 27, 1987.

. . .the Reagan administration's behavior was not only illegal, but also immoral.

"It's illegal, but what else is new?" is how the editor of a national magazine put it when I suggested a follow-up of a story the *National Catholic Reporter* had printed on questionable contributions to Reagan's 1980 presidential campaign.

Yet it was and is something more. In all the thousands of words written in the major media about the Iran-contra imbroglio, I have yet to see a discussion of the essence of the issue—that the Reagan administration's behavior was not only illegal, but also immoral.

Polls and surveys tell us our country is one of the most religious in the world because of the number of people who attend churches and synagogues or profess a religious belief. Yet, this same society turns a blind eye to white-collar crime—which is what the Iran-contra scandal is about—presumably because people who wear three-piece suits and attend church are in a different class from street thieves, even though white-collar criminals cause far more damage to our economy and political system. Such people do not commit crimes but are guilty of "illegalities," or legal mistakes.

Religious Codes

Our religious and civil codes teach us not to lie, but last fall the CIA's Catholic director, William Casey, was planning to lie to a Senate commission about the sale of U.S. arms to Iran. According to the Washington Post, Casey had intended to tell the commission that government authorities knew nothing about the delivery of U.S. antitank missiles by Israel to Iran. Casey changed his testimony, said the Post, only after Secretary of State George Shultz raised hell. Shultz may not be everybody's ideal, but he does understand the law. Even the State Department's high-powered lawyers would be hard put to find a legal precedent to justify the head of the CIA lying to Congress under oath. (Others had done it, of course, but they generally took care not to tell tales when public attention was focused on their every word.)

Casey's deviousness was typical of those involved in the scandal, from Reagan on down. They ignored U.S. laws in selling military equipment to Iran while destroying the antiterrorist pillar on which the Reagan administration's foreign policy had been founded. You may believe that they did so out of compassion for a few hostages in Lebanon, but I find that too

facile, as the president has never shown himself compassionate. Where is the logic in dealing with a government that held American diplomats hostage in Iran—remember how Reagan ranted against Carter's weak-kneed response to the Ayatollah Khomeini? What is the sense of providing American arms to a regime that financed terrorist attacks in Lebanon? Have we forgotten the massacre of our Marines there?

The explanation, if you want to buy it, is that the Reagan administration thought it could kill two birds with one stone by gaining influence with less-radical elements in the Iranian government and obtaining the release of hostages in Lebanon. By the by, the CIA's secret accounts in Switzerland, which were used to handle the arms sales to Iran, also served as a funnel to direct profits from the Iranian deal to the contras when Congress had prohibited government aid.

Money and Taxes

When all the smoke has cleared, we may discover that the main objective was not a few hostages in Lebanon but money for the "private" contra funding network, the principal White House liaison for which was Oliver North, also point man in the

Iranian negotiations.

How was the money spent? Among other things, it paid for the construction of an airstrip near the Costa Rican-Nicaraguan border that was used by contras working with the Colombian cocaine cartel to transship drugs to the United States. As shown by exhaustive investigations by U.S. journalists and congressional committees, contra involvement in drug smuggling was widespread. Even Elliott Abrams, the abrasive assistant secretary of state for inter-American affairs and contra champion, had to admit the reports were true, although he claimed the contras had been victimized by unscrupulous Columbian traffickers.

The bottom line is that our tax dollars were used to arm a government that has supported international terrorism and to facilitate the shipments of narcotics to our own country. Others may speak of this scandal in terms of "illegalities"—many of the recent opinion surveys are so worded. But an illegal act is still wrong.

CIA and Drugs

The worst of it, as my newspaper colleagues point out, is, "So what else is new?"

The CIA has long record of involvement in the drug traffic, dating to the war in Vietnam. Among those who worked with North on the contra operation were intelligence veterans of Vietnam and the CIA's secret war in Laos, where the CIA supported a Meo tribesmen army that was deeply involved in drug trafficking. The evidence also shows that the CIA ignored the drug activities of high-ranking officials of Nguyen Van Thieu's regime in South Vietnam despite the spread of heroin addiction among U.S. troops. Some of these same intelligence officials were also involved with the CIA's secret war against Fidel Castro, which included deals with the U.S. mafia.

Most of the Cuban exiles recruited for the war tried to make an honest buck on their return to civilian life, but a minority gained fame as the leaders of Miami's drug traffic. U.S. congressional and press investigations show that the Cuban Miami connection played an important role in contra drug-smuggling activities in Central America.

Begin at the beginning, we're told. Our postwar history is strewn with examples of government officials who could not discern the difference between right and wrong and whose only concern was to cover up "illegalities." We see countless variations on the theme in the marketplace, where "smart" business executives make a killing by bending the law. It's embarrassing to their supporters when they get caught, and sometimes costly, as Ivan Boesky's erstwhile partners have learned. But few seem to feel any concern about the ethics in question.

The contradiction in our society is obvious: How can we really be one of the most religious nations in the world if so many of us fail to act on our beliefs?

The Problem

No one has a magical solution to the problem, but I think one area we should pay more attention to is education. Numerous surveys have shown that students do not connect values with functional knowledge as, for example, engineering majors who separate "value-free" technology from "subjective" ethical beliefs, never seeing how the one can affect the other. Many teachers, psychiatrists and other professionals involved in education are embarrassed to use the word "moral," which has been replaced by "social," as in "the social development of children." Our public school textbooks are afraid to even mention religion—thus Christmas is "a warm time for special foods" and Thanksgiving reduced to "a pumpkin-pie party with the Indians."

If our educators are reluctant to speak about morality—if they are unwilling to admit that what is right can be known—we should not be surprised at the lack of morality in government, which is, after all, a reflection of the governed. No, there's "nothing new" in the Iran-contra scandal—Irangate, isn't it? What would be new is some old-fashioned moral indignation.

52

6   THE MIDDLE EAST ARMS BAZAAR

ARMS SALES TO IRAN: A WORTHWHILE EFFORT

Richard Cheney

The following article was excerpted from a minority report of the Congressional Committee Investigating the Iran-Contra Affair. Congressman Richard Cheney of Wyoming was the Ranking House Republican who organized the dissenting minority report.

Points to Consider:

1. Why were arms sold to Iran?

2. Who was Manucher Ghorbanifar and what role did he play?

3. In what ways is Iran important to the United States?

4. How was this importance related to arms sales?

Excerpted from the Report of the Congressional Committees Investigating the Iran-Contra Affair, November, 1987, pp. 519-24.

Without endorsing or agreeing with the use of arms sales as a tactic, we believe that U.S. officials made a risky, but nevertheless worthwhile effort.

The United States was taken by surprise when the Shah fell in 1979, because it had not developed an adequate human intelligence capability in Iran. Our hearings have established that little had been done to remedy the situation by the mid-1980s. The United States was still without adequate intelligence when, in 1985, it was approached by Israel with a proposal that the United States acquiesce in Israeli sales of U.S.-origin arms to Iran. This proposal came at a time when the National Security Council (NSC) was already circulating a recommendation that the United States consider the advisability of such sales to Iran. Long term strategic considerations dictated that the United States try to improve relations with at least some of the important factions in Iran. The lack of adequate intelligence about the situation inside Iran made it imperative to pursue potentially fruitful opportunity; it also made those pursuits inherently risky. United States decisions of necessity had to be based on the thinnest of independently verifiable information. Lacking such independent intelligence, the United States was forced to rely on sources known to be biased and unreliable. Well aware of the risk, the Administration nonetheless decided that the opportunity was worth pursuing.

An Opening

To explore the chance for an opening, the President decided to sell arms to Iran. Some suggest that this decision stemmed from little more than the President's ignorance, the NSC staff's foolhardiness, and private greed. We completely reject this interpretation. The initiative was controversial. We disagree with the decision to sell arms, and we wish that the whole initiative had proceeded with more caution. But despite these reservations, we remain convinced that the decision to pursue some such initiative was not an inherently unreasonable one.

The major participants in the Iran arms affair obviously had some common and some conflicting interests. The key question the United States had to explore was whether the U.S. and Iranian leadership actually felt enough of a common interest to establish a strategic dialogue. No one can deny the common U.S. and Iranian interest in opposing Soviet expansion. But how much would that community of interest be felt, acknowledged and acted upon? Iran and the United States have compatible

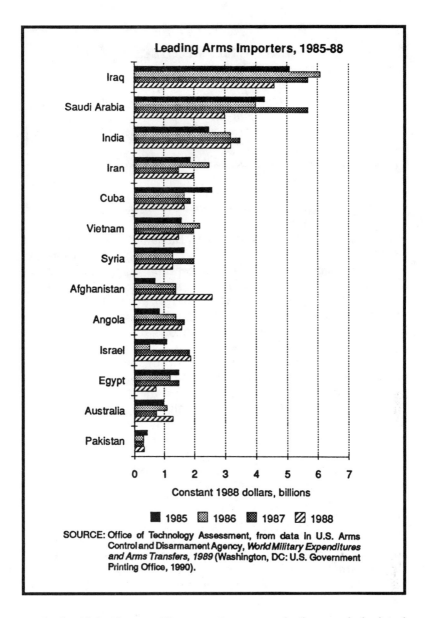

Leading Arms Importers, 1985-88

Iraq
Saudi Arabia
India
Iran
Cuba
Vietnam
Syria
Afghanistan
Angola
Israel
Egypt
Australia
Pakistan

0 1 2 3 4 5 6 7

Constant 1988 dollars, billions

■ 1985 ▦ 1986 ▨ 1987 ▨ 1988

SOURCE: Office of Technology Assessment, from data in U.S. Arms
Control and Disarmament Agency, *World Military Expenditures
and Arms Transfers, 1989* (Washington, DC: U.S. Government
Printing Office, 1990).

goals in Afghanistan. The question was whether such isolated
examples could be broadened into something more substantial.

Ghorbanifar

The initial dealings with the Iranian government were
undermined by the unreliability of the intermediary, Manucher
Ghorbanifar. Nevertheless, Ghorbanifar did help obtain the

release of two U.S. hostages (Rev. Benjamin Weir and Father Lawrence Jenco) and he did also produce high Iranian officials for the first face to face meetings between our governments in five years. At those meetings, U.S. officials sought consistently to make clear that we were interested in a long-term strategic relationship with Iran to oppose Soviet expansionism. The hostages issue was presented as an obstacle to an enhanced relationship that would have to be overcome, not as the objective of the initiative. Colonel North made an extensive presentation to this effect in February 1986; former National Security Adviser McFarlane made a similar presentation in Tehran in May 1986. But the Iranian officials brought by Ghorbanifar seemed to be interested only in weapons, and in using the hostages for bargaining leverage. The full extent of the difference between these approaches finally was made obvious to the United States at the meeting in Tehran, which North, McFarlane and others attended at great personal risk.

Hakim

After the Tehran meetings, the United States was able to approach a very high-ranking Iranian official using a second channel arranged by Albert Hakim and his associates. Clearly, Hakim had business motives in arranging these contacts. Whatever his motives, he did produce contacts at the highest levels of the Iranian government. Discussions with this channel began in the middle of 1986 and continued until December. They resulted in the release of one further hostage (David Jacobsen), and U.S. officials expected them to result in the release of more hostages. Perhaps more importantly, these discussions appear to have considered the possibility of broad areas of strategic cooperation. However, as a result of factional infighting inside the Iranian government, the initiative was

56

exposed and substantive discussions were suspended. Not surprisingly, given the nature of Iranian politics, the Iranian government has publicly denied that significant negotiations had taken place.

The Iran Initiative

The Reagan Administration's Iran initiative represented an attempt to narrow the differences stemming from the Iranian revolution and the intervening years of hostility. Both sides confronted sharp internal divisions over the issue of rapprochement. In such a situation, the margin between success and failure looms much larger in retrospect than it may seem while events are unfolding.

In retrospect, it seems clear that this initiative degenerated into a series of "arms for hostage" deals. But it did not look that way to many of the U.S. participants at the time. In our view, it is simply wrong, therefore, to reduce the complex motivations behind these events to any one simple thesis. Clearly, the participants from different countries, and even those within each country, had different, and sometimes conflicting, motives. Without endorsing or agreeing with the use of arms sales as a tactic, we believe that U.S. officials made a risky, but nevertheless worthwhile effort. To explain why, we shall begin by outlining the strategic importance of Iran.

The Strategic Context

Iran is the largest country in the Persian Gulf region, an area of vital economic importance to the United States and its allies. It is in a strategic position potentially to dominate the world's largest proven oil reserves and threaten the vulnerable pro-Western states of the Gulf.

Iran dominates the entire eastern shore of the Persian Gulf; it controls the Strait of Hormuz and can threaten the free flow of oil from the Gulf to the industrial economies of the West. In 1987, as part of its effort to disrupt non-Iranian shipping traffic in the Gulf, Iran has used anti-ship missiles and other munitions to attack neutral oil tankers, and laid mines throughout the Gulf. U.S. and allied warships have been deployed in the Gulf to ensure that the flow of oil is not impeded. Although less than six percent of U.S. oil consumption transits the Gulf, 24 percent of Western Europe's oil and almost half of Japan's total oil consumption must pass through the Strait of Hormuz. Iran alone supplies some five percent of Western Europe's and Japan's oil. Increased oil production elsewhere in the world,

57

and the opening of new pipelines to take oil through Turkey, Iran and Saudi Arabia have somewhat reduced the Gulf's relative importance. Even so, Iran remains able to be a seriously disruptive force to the world's economy.

In addition to its importance to oil supplies and oil routes, Iran, whose population of about 45 million is larger than the other Gulf states combined, is in a position to dominate or destabilize the small, weak, pro-Western countries of the Western Gulf coastal region. Recent Iranian policy toward Kuwait exemplifies the pressure Iran can exert on its neighbors. An aggressive Iran can promote anti-Western Shiite fundamentalism throughout the Middle East, threatening key U.S. allies such as Israel, Egypt, and Turkey.

The majority report systematically downplays the importance of strategic objectives in the Iran initiative. We believe, to the contrary, that the record is unambiguous on the following facts: (1) that strategic objectives were important to the participants at all times; (2) that the objectives were credible, (3) that they were the driving force for the initiative at the outset, and (4) that without such a strategic concern, the initiative would never have been undertaken.

As we said earlier, one need not agree with these strategic goals, or agree that arms sales were a good way to achieve them, to recognize their importance to the key players. The Administration felt it was crucial to begin making some inroads into Iran, before that country became embroiled in a succession crisis. It was important to keep looking for opportunities. Unfortunately, our ignorance of the situation in Iran was such that we had few realistic ways to do so.

7   THE MIDDLE EAST ARMS BAZAAR

PROMOTING A MIDDLE EAST ARMS RACE

Frank Greve and Susan Bennett

Frank Greve and Susan Bennett wrote this article for the Knight-Ridder *News Service. The following article was reprinted from the* Saint Paul Pioneer Press.

Points to Consider:

1. How is the New World Order defined?

2. Why does the Pentagon like the new "arms for allies policy"?

3. How might arms sales undermine governments in the Middle East?

4. How is the relationship between oil and arms explained by the author?

5. What is the real reason for arms sales to the Middle East?

Frank Greve and Susan Bennett, "New World Order Arms for Oil Allies," **Saint Paul Pioneer Press**, July 7, 1991. Reprinted by permission of **Knight-Ridder Tribune News.**

"The main purpose for military sales to the region has always been the money involved."

Saudi Arabia is buying from the United States billions of dollars worth of weapons that its troops don't need.

What the Saudis do need is the exclusive warranty that comes with the goods: Buy American arms and you buy American protection. If there is a New World Order in the Persian Gulf, that's it.

Since August, the U.S. arms-for-allies policy has extracted more than $34 billion in weapons orders from the region. These sales—and the tighter strategic alliance that they cement—deliver immediate economic gains. But they also entail long-term commitments of U.S. troops to defend corrupt and feudal monarchies in an unstable region.

For now, the marriage of the world's leading military power and the leading oil powers most excites American defense contractors and lawmakers from defense-dependent districts. They face an otherwise sluggish global arms market and sharp domestic defense spending cuts.

It also heartens Pentagon brass. They figure exports will keep U.S. defense plants going at no cost to their budgets while offering new missions in Saudi Arabia to replace their fading European roles.

And, since the new alliance includes assurances of cheap Persian Gulf oil, it has non-military appeal for a nation that runs on cheap oil.

But for all its advantages, American experts on the Arab world wonder how the alliance will be tested, as marriages inevitably are.

Mostly, they worry that the infusion of U.S. arms and influence will destabilize Saudi Arabia, just as it once destabilized another Persian Gulf oil monarchy, Iran.

History

"We have a very unfortunate history of making the most sophisticated arms deliveries to governments which, although they happen to be stable at the moment, prove to be unstable," warns Tom Lantos of California, a senior Democrat on the House Foreign Affairs Committee.

Among the troubling possibilities, analysts believe, are these:

- Ecoterrorism and missile attacks worked well for Iraq while

Arms Deals Up In Bush Administration

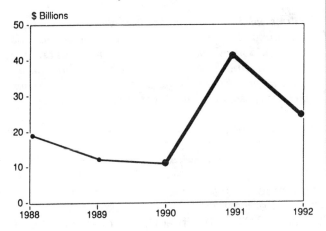

$ Billions

Includes government and commercial sales, training and surplus sales.
1990 estimated, 1991-92 projected.
Sources: DOD, State Dept., CDI.

Chart prepared by Center for Defense Information

traditional ground forces performed dismally. So the next challenge—from whatever quarter—is likely to be unconventional and tougher.

- Forty years of "defensive" arming of the Middle East have made the region no less tense but a lot more dangerous. More arms can hardly help.

- So long as Persian Gulf leaders appear to be players on an American infidel team, their legitimacy in Muslim eyes will erode.

- Defending Saudi Arabia and its allies entails defending corrupt monarchies. Absent a threat as Hitlerian as Saddam Hussein, Americans may not be keen to save billionaire kings and emirs.

And clearly the Bush administration has pledged that U.S. troops will step in when local forces falter.

"In the long run, we must provide the capabilities the countries in the region cannot provide," said Paul Wolfowitz, Undersecretary of Defense in testimony last fall before the House Foreign Affairs Committee.

But mounting an adequate expeditionary force could be difficult, worries Patrick Clawson, director of the Foreign Policy Research Institute of Philadelphia, given planned defense cuts and "particularly if our strategy is the same next time: to overwhelm the foe with a huge military force."

Moreover, if past is prologue, U.S. troops can expect to do most of the fighting in a virtually mercenary relationship.

Military Roles

Amateurish performances in the Gulf War prompted American Desert Storm veterans to dub their Arab allies "speed bumps": troops sure to be overrun by advancing armies.

Still, Persian Gulf allies have military roles to play, Wolfowitz insisted, and "we should not do for them what they can do for themselves."

For their self-defense, Wolfowitz strongly recommended U.S. arms. As he put it, "Standardization on U.S. equipment promotes the ability of local armed forces to operate more effectively with U.S. units should reinforcement of the region be needed again in the future."

Persian Gulf states got the message. Their leaders met with Defense Secretary Dick Cheney in early May and are meeting now with a Pentagon team to develop a comprehensive regional defense package that could be worth more than $20 billion to U.S. arms manufacturers in the '90s.

Already, $7 billion in debt forgiveness for Egypt for past arms purchases, $1.6 billion in new Egyptian arms deals, encouragement of new Israeli purchases, and $7 billion in sales to the Saudis are heating the market.

The Saudis

The Saudis would like to order an additional $14 billion in more controversial wares, including additional AWACs, midair refueling aircraft and missiles. When Congress heard Israeli alarms and sounded resistant last October, this package was split off from the original $21 billion order Cheney brought home.

If it resurfaces, the Saudis will supplant Iraq as the decade's leading arms buyer and the United States could overtake the flagging Soviet Union as the world's leading seller.

Currently, U.S. sales account for only about 30 percent of Saudi arms deliveries, according to a Library of Congress study. Britain has the lion's share, thanks to aircraft sales that began in 1985 after Congress refused, under heavy pressure from Israel's friends, to sell advanced fighters to the Saudis.

The stakes for the United States are enormous. Approved and pending sales to Saudi Arabia of tanks, fighting vehicles and armored cars, for example, will keep open U.S. production lines that otherwise would be shutting down.

Proposed Saudi tank sales alone will yield 68,900 job-years in Michigan, Indiana, California, Connecticut and Ohio, based on Defense Department figures offered in congressional testimony.

Not to be forgotten is that Persian Gulf arms sales are for cash, unlike arms transfers to most allies, including Egypt and Israel, that require U.S. credit, notes William Rope, an official of the Defense Department's Bureau of Political-Military Affairs.

With help from arms sales, the United States could continue to have a favorable balance of payments with the region despite oil imports that reached $15 billion last year.

To keep oil prices low, Saudi Arabia has single-handedly replaced lost Kuwaiti and Iraqi oil with 2 million barrels a day from its surplus capacity. King Fahd took that step August 6, 1990 the day Cheney left Riyadh with Fahd's invitation to American defenders.

So heady are the benefits that the most puzzling aspect of the new security deal is easily overlooked: the basic weakness of Saudi ground force leadership, training and determination.

Aside from the elite Saudi air force, dominated by flyboy princes, analysts dismiss Persian Gulf troops as too inept to use sophisticated weapons in sophisticated ways.

But that fact, when turned on its head, suits the alliance perfectly: If Saudi defenders are feckless, Americans who benefit from the House of Saud's dependency need not worry that capable Saudi troops will supplant them in military roles, and the ever-nervous House of Saud need not worry about a military coup.

Royal Family

"It's a subtle scam," said a retired Army officer who has served in Saudi Arabia and trained Saudi ground troops. "At some level, we don't want them to be competent, and at some level, THEY don't want them to be competent."

At the same time, the Saudi royal family has much to gain—personally—from buying arms. Three of Fahd's brothers are rivals for largess—Crown Prince Abdullah, head of the national guard; Prince Sultan, minister of defense and aviation; and Prince Naif, minister of interior.

King Fahd, who bestows the favors, expects subcontracts to be distributed among friends and family, according to American arms dealers to the kingdom who asked not to be named. The spoils promote loyalty to the leader, rather like a city political machine.

In the latest Saudi arms deals, everybody wins. Prince Sultan's forces and factions get new General Dynamics M-1A2 tanks. Abdullah's national guard gets new General Motors light armored vehicles. While Prince Naif appears left out, a son, Prince Saud, was a founding stockholder in the General Dynamics subsidiary that will maintain Sultan's tanks, according to a published 1984 registration.

How well will upgraded armored units perform? "Truck drivers earn three times the pay of army conscripts in Saudi Arabia," the Persian Gulf diplomat replied, "How well do you expect them to drive tanks?"

So analysts laugh when asked about the bang-for-the-buck from Saudi arms sales. "The main purpose for military sales to the region has always been the money involved," James Akins, former U.S. ambassador to Saudi Arabia, observes dryly.

8   THE MIDDLE EAST ARMS BAZAAR

CURBING MIDDLE EAST ARMS SALES

U.S. State Department

The following public paper by the U.S. State Department describes the Middle East Arms Control Initiative made by President Bush on May 29, 1991.

Points to Consider:

1. What is the purpose of the new proposal from the President?

2. How will the new proposal restrain an arms race in the Middle East?

3. What kind of arms trade will be permitted under this new proposal?

4. How would nuclear weapons be dealt with?

5. How would chemical and biological weapons be dealt with?

Excerpted from a public paper released by the U.S. State Department, May 29, 1991.

Since proliferation is a global problem, it must find a global solution.

Fulfilling the pledge he made in his March 6, 1991 address to a joint session of Congress, the President announced a series of proposals intended to curb the spread of nuclear, chemical and biological weapons in the Middle East, as well as the missiles that can deliver them. The proposals also seek to restrain a destabilizing conventional arms build-up in the region.

The proposals would apply to the entire Middle East, including Iraq, Iran, Libya, Syria, Egypt, Lebanon, Israel, Jordan, Saudi Arabia, and the other states of the Maghreb and the Gulf Cooperation Council. They reflect our consultations with allies, governments in the region, and key suppliers of arms and technology.

The support of both exporters and importers will be essential to the success of the initiative. Since proliferation is a global problem, it must find a global solution. At the same time, the current situation in the Middle East poses unique dangers and opportunities. Thus, the President's proposal will concentrate on the Middle East as its starting point, while complementing other initiatives such as those taken by Prime Ministers John Major and Brian Mulroney. It includes the following elements.

Supplier Restraint

The initiative calls on the five major suppliers of conventional arms to meet at senior levels in the near future to discuss the establishment of guidelines for restraints on destabilizing transfers of conventional arms, as well as weapons of mass destruction and associated technology. France has agreed to host the initial meeting. (The United Kingdom, France, the Soviet Union, China, and the United States have supplied the vast majority of the conventional arms exported to the Middle East in the last decade.) At the same time, these guidelines will permit states in the region to acquire the conventional capabilities they legitimately need to deter and defend against military aggression.

- These discussions will be expanded to include other suppliers in order to obtain the broadest possible cooperation. The London Summit of the G-7, to be hosted by the British in July, 1991, will provide an early opportunity to begin to engage other governments.

- To implement this regime, the suppliers would commit

66

"I told the man at the U.S. Embassy we needed help to farm the area, but I think he thought I said 'bomb the area.'"

—to observe a general code of responsible arms transfers;

—to avoid destabilizing transfers; and

—to establish effective domestic export controls on the end-use of arms or other items to be transferred.

● The guidelines will include a mechanism for consultations among suppliers, who would

—notify one another in advance of certain arms sales;

—meet regularly to consult on arms transfers;

—consult on an ad hoc basis if a supplier believed guidelines were not being observed; and

—provide one another with an annual report on transfers.

Missiles

The initiative proposes a freeze on the acquisition, production, and testing of surface-to-surface missiles by states in the region with a view to the ultimate elimination of such missiles from their arsenals.

- Suppliers would also step up efforts to coordinate export licensing for equipment, technology and services that could be used to manufacture surface-to-surface missiles. Export licenses would be provided only for peaceful end uses.

The initiative builds on existing institutions and focuses on activities directly related to nuclear weapons capability. The initiative would

- Call on regional states to implement a verifiable ban on the production and acquisition of weapons-usable nuclear material (enriched uranium or separated plutonium);
- Reiterate our call on all states in the region that have not already done so to accede to the Non-Proliferation Treaty;
- Reiterate our call to place all nuclear facilities in the region under International Atomic Energy Agency safeguards; and
- Continue to support the eventual creation of a regional nuclear weapon-free zone.

Chemical Weapons

The proposal will build on the President's recent initiative to achieve early completion of the global Chemical Weapons Convention.

- The initiative calls for all states in the region to commit to becoming original parties to the Convention.

- Given the history of possession and use of chemical weapons in the region, the initiative also calls for regional states to institute confidence-building measures now by engaging in presignature implementation of appropriate Chemical Weapons Convention provisions.

Biological Weapons

As with the approach to chemical weapon controls, the proposals build on an existing global approach. The initiative would

- Call for strengthening the 1972 Biological Weapons Convention (BWC) through full implementation of existing BWC provisions and an improved mechanism for information exchange. These measures will be pursued at the five-year Review Conference of the BWC this September, 1991.

- Urge regional states to adopt biological weapons confidence-building measures.

This initiative complements our continuing support for the continuation of the U.N. Security Council embargo against arms transfers to Iraq, as well as the efforts of the U.N. Special Commission to eliminate Iraq's remaining capabilities to use or produce nuclear, chemical, and biological weapons and the missiles to deliver them.

THE MIDDLE EAST ARMS BAZAAR

THE ARMING OF IRAQ:
A CASE STUDY

Tom Hamburger

Tom Hamburger is the Washington D.C. Bureau Chief for the Minneapolis Star Tribune.

Points to Consider:

1. From the reading, prepare a list of items sold by the U.S. to Iraq. Include the costs when given.

2. What types of facilities did the U.S. and Germany plan to construct in Iraq prior to the August, 1990 invasion of Kuwait?

3. Why is the sale of sophisticated computer technology so potentially dangerous? Give examples.

Tom Hamburger, "U.S. to Blame for Iraq's Arsenal of Weapons," **Star Tribune** of Minneapolis, January 14, 1991. Reprinted with permission of the **Star Tribune**, Minneapolis-St. Paul..

German, Austrian, British and firms from 20 other countries provided a long list of machinery for weapons manufacture in Iraq.

From the mid-1980s until Iraq invaded Kuwait this past summer, the United States and other Western countries knowingly and unknowingly aided Saddam Hussein's program to build one of the world's most powerful arsenals. Companies ranging from Unisys Inc. in Minnesota to a tiny cherry-flavoring factory in Florida may have played a role in Hussein's schemes.

Sometimes the help came through Iraq's covert arms-buying network—dozens of agents and front companies that bought or stole strategic materials from industrial countries around the globe.

More often, strategic goods were shipped with the blessing of U.S. export-control officials. Since 1985, nearly 700 licenses for shipments of $1.5 billion worth of goods with both military and domestic applications have been authorized to Iraq. Critics contend that those shipments advanced Iraq's nuclear, chemical and conventional weapons ambitions.

Hussein has worked deliberately in recent years to build self-sufficiency in arms-making. At the time of the invasion of Kuwait, U.S. and German firms were negotiating to build plants that would help him achieve this self-sufficiency.

Centrifugal Casting Machine Co. of Tulsa, Oklahoma, had a $26 million contract to place machine tools in a factory owned by BADR Industries, Iraq's largest manufacturer of bombs, according to a Paris-based military analyst Ken Timmerman. The contract was never fulfilled, said company spokesman Tom McKee, and a lawsuit is pending to resolve contract questions. He declined to comment further on the contract. Asked whether the contract would have provided help to Iraqi weapons manufacturers, he said only that "your information is not correct."

U.S. Policy Tilt

Before the Iran-Iraq war in 1980, the United States had an arms embargo in effect against Iraq. Then the U.S. decided to "tilt" toward Iraq, and a wide variety of potentially useful materials began to flow. None were supposed to have direct military application without special approval from the State Department.

In the mid-1980s, 45 Bell-214 helicopters were sent to Iraq

RPS·1991

despite objections that the chopper is easily converted to military use.

Rep. Howard Berman, D-Calif., was one of several legislators and Pentagon officials who protested that the helicopters had a clear military application. "It is beyond belief that Iraq. . .would purchase 45 helicopters at $5 million each simply to transport 'civilian VIPs,'" he wrote the secretary of state.

Nonetheless, the sale went through, just as the sale of 60 Hughes helicopters had the year before. Those helicopters were used to train Iraqi pilots and were the kind the U.S. Army uses for scouting, Berman said.

The United States was not alone in satisfying Hussein's appetite for military goods. German, Austrian, British and firms from 20 other countries provided a long list of machinery for weapons manufacture in Iraq. And the Soviets provided weapons outright.

Americans led the way in providing computers to help Hussein towards his most desired goal, nuclear weapons. At Iraq's Sa'ad 16 research center for missile and nuclear weaponry near Mosul, most of the computer equipment was U.S. made, said former Deputy Undersecretary of Defense Stephen Bryen. Most of the equipment sales were approved by the U.S.

SWEDEN EXPORTS ARMS

If the past is any guide, a bill which would further restrict the possibilities for Swedish military exports and cooperation should not be expected. Within both the government and the military economy, strong support exists for sustained military production. The result has been an "armament race", not with another nation, but within the industry itself.

Thus, there is no automatic link between Swedish armament behavior and reduced political tension in Europe. In order to be affordable in the short term, the arms industry relies increasingly on international trade.

Bjorn Hagelin, **The New Economy**, February, 1991

government despite objections from the Pentagon. For example, the Pentagon repeatedly objected to the sale of a $450,000 computer built by Electronics Associates of Long Branch, New Jersey. The computer is similar to those used in velocity tests at White Sands missile range in New Mexico. It was shipped to Iraq just before the invasion of Kuwait and has now been installed, Bryen said. Company officials had no comment.

A Hewlett Packard computer system was licensed for sale to the Iraqis last year and is now in use at the Sa'ad site, according to congressional military analysts. The company has acknowledged the sale to Iraq but said it had no confirmation that the computer had been used for military purposes. The Iraqis bought several computers made by U.S. companies in recent years. None has been shown to have been used by the military. Bryen opposed sale of all computers to the Iraqi government.

A review of Commerce Department licenses by the *Minneapolis Star Tribune* showed that Unisys sold a $500,000 computer to the Iraqi Defense Ministry last year, ostensibly for use in payroll and accounting. A few years ago, the company sold a $8.7 million computer package to the Interior Ministry. The sale met all government requirements and served no military purpose, said Unisys spokeswoman Laura Overstreet.

A $350,000 Honeywell computer was sold to the Ministry of Industry and Minerals in late 1988. Other sales from the Commerce files that could benefit Iraq's nuclear effort: A $661,875 sale of computing equipment and electronics for "isotopic abundances and radio elements" to Iraq's Ministry of Heavy Industry; an oven that can be used "to prepare fissionable material for use in a nuclear device;" computers used by the Atomic Energy Commission "for use with existing equipment for gamma-gamma conciliation."

These licenses were not isolated cases. They were part of a tidal wave of technical assistance provided to Iraq in recent years, despite warnings that the country was aggressive, supported terrorism and was building a nuclear weapons capability. Bryen said that licenses also had been granted for U.S. technical equipment needed "to repair rocket casings."

Iraqi chemical weapons architect Ihsan Barbouti invested $5 million in a Florida cherry-flavoring plant, Product Ingredient Technology Inc., in an apparent effort to obtain cyanide compounds. It was one of a long string of investments Barbouti made in companies that could help export strategic goods to Iraq.

The president of the Boca Raton Company, Louis Champon, told reporters in Florida he had no idea that the Iraqi investor was interested in his company to export a weapons ingredient. He has acknowledged to reporters that several barrels of a cyanide complex were missing from his plant, which makes ingredients for food and soft drinks.

Most Disturbing Sales

If biological weapons are used, the cultures also may have been developed with the help of U.S. firms.

A company called American Type Cultures of Rockville, Maryland, sent bacteria strains to Iraq, according to Commerce records. A company official, Bobbi Brandon, declined to comment, referring all questions to the Commerce Department. Commerce officials had no comment.

Another firm sold "bacteria, protozoa and fungi for scientific research" to Iraq in April 1988. Said Bryen: "I don't know why they sent them there or why it was approved by Commerce. Saddam Hussein is not the sort of end user one normally sends biological samples for humanitarian or peaceful purposes."

With chemical, biological, conventional and maybe even nuclear warheads in place, U.S. technology was there to help guide these weapons on their way.

One of the most disturbing sales in the Commerce Department files is the transfer of "computer enhanced photographic equipment" to Iraq, said Bryen. Officially, the license for International Imaging Systems of Milpitas, California, said that its equipment would be used for Iraq's Astronomy Research Center at Mosul.

The license application was viewed skeptically by Bryen, who headed the Defense Technical Security Agency. The equipment, he said, could be used for targeting missiles and for surveillance from airplanes and satellites. U.S. cruise missiles are guided by such systems.

"It was a hard-fought bureaucratic battle," said Bryen, who thought he had won the battle by taking it to the White House until a military analyst reported that the system was en route to Iraq.

Company Vice President Anthony Musladin said his firm complied with all regulations and that the system was "decontrolled and nonstrategic."

Bryen disagreed: "It's quite possible they could have used this equipment to track our forces in the desert, our ships in the gulf or to guide missiles more precisely against Americans."

EXAMINING COUNTERPOINTS

This activity may be used as an individualized study guide for students in libraries and resource centers or as a discussion catalyst in small group and classroom discussions.

The Point

The Iran-Contra affair was both illegal and immoral. Tax dollars were used to arm a government that supported terrorism. Profits generated from arms sales to Iran were then used to arm the Nicaraguan Contras, a policy prohibited by the Congress. "Illegalities" were covered up with no regard for what was right or wrong.

The Counterpoint

The Iran-Contra affair was neither illegal nor immoral. Pledges must occasionally be broken in the interests of national security. Arms deals with Iran were justified in order to free American hostages and to support the Contras against the leftist government in Nicaragua. By avoiding direct U.S. government assistance, the law was upheld.

Guidelines

Social issues are usually complex, but often problems become oversimplified in political debates and discussion. Usually a polarized version of social conflict does not adequately represent the diversity of views that surround social conflicts.

Examine the counterpoints above. Then write down possible interpretations of this issue other than the two arguments stated in the counterpoints above.

CHAPTER 4

CURBING WORLD ARMS SALES: IDEAS IN CONFLICT

ARMS SALES AND GLOBAL EXPLOITATION

Dolores Taller

Dolores Taller is chairperson of the Middle East Committee of The Women's International League for Peace and Freedom (WILPF).

Points to Consider:

1. What are "surrogates"? Give several specific examples.

2. What is the inevitable result of arms sales to Third World countries by the superpowers.

3. Who are the primary victims of the global arms trade? Who profits the most?

4. How does U.S. aid in the Middle East actually prevent a peace settlement?

Dolores Taller "Arms Sales, Military Aid and U.S. Intervention," **Peace and Freedom,** June, 1988.

Miltary aid and arms sales are obstacles to peaceful settlement of conflicts throughout the world.

The United States uses military aid and arms sales as major tools in the effort to protect U.S. "national interests". In the 1988 report of the Commission on Integrated Long Term Strategy, Henry Kissinger and others note that in the future, nuclear warfare in Europe is less likely than conflicts between the U.S. and poor nations over resources. Therefore, the report says, the Third World must be the main target of U.S. military planning.

Since the 1940s, Washington has focused its concern on nationalist leaders who are potential allies of the Soviet Union and might challenge U.S. interests. Immediately after World War II, to gain domestic support for opposing these forces, the Truman Doctrine portrayed conflicts all over the world as part of the global struggle "between Western freedom and Soviet tyranny." The U.S. has used variations on this theme ever since to justify its military policy.

Surrogates

The U.S. has intervened through arms sales and military aid particularly in situations where it finds the use of surrogates more appropriate than direct U.S. military action. Such an approach has in the past been followed by direct U.S. military intervention, such as occurred in Vietnam.

U.S. policy around the world is to support a leader or administration who will be pro-U.S. or anti-communist, whether or not the regime is democratic. The U.S. provides arms and military training to prevent "radical" new leaders from taking power in a country, or to enable it to intervene in neighboring states should an "unwelcome" change in government take place. During the 1970s, for example, the U.S. armed the Shah of Iran to maintain control of Iranian oil and the oil of the Arab Gulf states.

These surrogate relationships draw other countries into our strategic alliances to prevent unwanted social, political, or economic change. They are used where U.S. domestic opposition or local anti-Americanism would prevent direct U.S. involvement. Former government official Charles Waterman describes surrogates as a relatively cheap and "wondrous weapon" of U.S. foreign policy. He notes Israel's role in selling arms and providing funding for the Nicaraguan contras and Angolan rebels in return for the sale of sophisticated surveillance

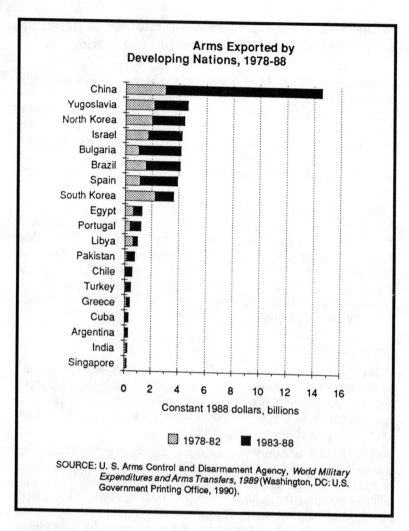

Arms Exported by Developing Nations, 1978-88

China
Yugoslavia
North Korea
Israel
Bulgaria
Brazil
Spain
South Korea
Egypt
Portugal
Libya
Pakistan
Chile
Turkey
Greece
Cuba
Argentina
India
Singapore

0 2 4 6 8 10 12 14 16

Constant 1988 dollars, billions

▦ 1978-82 ■ 1983-88

SOURCE: U. S. Arms Control and Disarmament Agency, *World Military Expenditures and Arms Transfers, 1989* (Washington, DC: U.S. Government Printing Office, 1990).

planes.

Where the U.S. plans for direct intervention, arms sales and military aid are incentives for countries in the region to accept U.S. bases. Following the downfall of the Shah of Iran and the Soviet invasion of Afghanistan, Presidents Carter and Reagan implemented plans for a mobile interventionary force now known as the Central Command.

Targeting Local Movements

Military aid and arms sales have been used by the Reagan administration to overthrow "pro-Soviet" regimes around the world through the support of insurgencies in Afghanistan, Angola, Cambodia, Nicaragua and elsewhere. Many of these activities were or are being carried out through the CIA and, as we now know, through the "private" networks revealed in the Iran-Contra scandal.

In reviewing these conflicts, arms analyst Michael Klare argues that the U.S. cannot permanently prevail against nationalist movements which deal with the concerns of local people. The causes of instability in a given area are deep in its political and social fabric. U.S. military aid and arms sales generally exacerbate the problems and often turn the people against the U.S. and its local surrogates. This leads to greater instability and often war. According to Klare, history shows that when a superpower engages in a continued military buildup in a Third World conflict, it will inevitably become directly involved.

Profits

While the main goals of interventionist U.S. policies are control of the resources and terms of trade in a region, arms sales also provide considerable profit for dealers and manufacturers. As our economy becomes increasingly based on military production, pressure grows to maintain the status quo.

While intervention through the arms trade and military aid is carried out by other nations, the U.S. and the Soviet Union together sell over half the arms worldwide. From 1970 to 1983,

Third World imports of arms increased by 742 percent, to a peak of $28 billion in 1983. Of the top 10 arms spenders, 7 are in the Middle East.

U.S.-provided aid to other countries for purchase of U.S. weapons in fiscal year 1988 is 62 percent above 1981 levels, with Egypt and Israel getting 41 percent, and about 25 percent going to Pakistan, Turkey, and the Philippines. In contrast, the amount of worldwide U.S. development aid since 1980 has changed little.

Impact: Human Suffering

Civilians suffer more in countries which spend the most on arms purchases and the military, because of decreased spending on social welfare programs, lower economic investment, higher taxes, inflation, and debt burden. Approximately 25 percent of the national debt in developing countries is due to arms imports.

The U.S. recognizes this relationship and provides so-called Economic Support Funds to Israel, El Salvador, Turkey, Egypt and other countries to counteract the negative effect on their economies. Nevertheless, Third World debt today exceeds the total amount of aid received, and these countries may never catch up. A vicious cycle is created: resources spent for arms leads to deteriorating human conditions, leading to increased political tensions and unrest, increased repression and violence, and more arms purchases.

Between internal conflicts and wars between neighbors, 50 countries are at war today. Over three-quarters of the victims are women and children. Swedish WILPF consultant Inge Thorssen warns: "Not to grasp the wider implications of these issues may well amount to a central misperception of our times."

Dangers and Obstacles to Peace

The danger is great today. Israeli nuclear technician Mordechai Vanunu has revealed that Israel has 100-200 nuclear weapons; U.S. and Soviet fleets in the Persian Gulf and Mediterranean carry nuclear-capable warheads. Pakistan and India are creating the ability to build nuclear weapons.

Military aid and arms sales are obstacles to peaceful settlement of conflicts throughout the world. Military aid from the U.S. or through surrogates to Guatemala, El Salvador, Honduras, Costa Rica and the Contras has undermined first the Contadora process, and now the Arias Plan. This aid keeps the military in control behind the supposedly civilian-ruled governments in Guatemala, El Salvador and elsewhere. The result has been terror and war against civilians.

The role of U.S. aid and arms in preventing a peace settlement of the Israeli-Arab/Palestinian conflict is more complex. U.S. aid helps Israel maintain its occupation of the West Bank and Gaza by offsetting funds for other purposes. U.S. arms sales to both sides stimulate the arms race between Israel and its Arab neighbors.

Middle East scholar Irene Gendzier notes that U.S. policies are not meant to end the Israeli-Palestinian conflict, but to maintain a certain level of stability in the region by warding off any "radical" liberation movement such as the PLO (Palestinian Liberation Organization). They are also aimed at strengthening U.S. influence in the Middle East and elsewhere through Middle East surrogates. For example, the Israeli-Egyptian peace treaty was followed by more than $5 billion in U.S. military aid and loans to Israel and Egypt. Since the treaty was signed, Egypt has been the site for military exercises by the U.S. Central Command, and Israel and the U.S. have signed agreements for air bases and for stockpiling U.S. equipment.

Israel's rejection of proposals for negotiation offers a lesson in the pitfalls of U.S. policy. Because the U.S. considers Israel to be a vital strategic ally, it is unwilling to use economic leverage to redirect Israeli policy. As long as strategic considerations are foremost, the U.S. is vulnerable to the decisions of the strategic client.

The alternative to intervention is a change in U.S. foreign policy. We must cooperate with others to end the global arms trade, seek negotiated settlements of conflicts, and build a new global economic order.

CONTROLLING THE SPREAD OF WEAPONS

U.S. Department of State

The following article was excerpted from a position paper presented to the Foreign Operations Subcommittee of the Senate Appropriations Committee.

Points to Consider:

1. How will security assistance (arms sales and military aid) contribute to peace?

2. Why does military aid promote arms control?

3. What Middle Eastern nations receive military arms and military aid from the U.S.?

4. Why do Latin American nations need military aid and arms?

Excerpted from a U.S. Department of State position paper, June 11, 1991.

The reality is that, for the foreseeable future, assuring stability—and enabling our friends to protect themselves—will require that we continue to provide arms and related services and training when and where appropriate.

Both Congress and the Administration recognize that our foreign aid program is one of the principal tools we have to advance our interest and objectives abroad. Today I want to examine how the use of one set of our foreign assistance tools—security assistance (arms and military aid)—contributes to our broad foreign policy goals: to preserve and protect peace and stability among nations and to promote democracy and development within them. In particular I want to discuss security assistance as it relates to two other key elements in our national security web: the fostering and maintenance of our alliances and the advancement of our arms control and non-proliferation agendas.

Promote and Maintain Collective Self-Defense Arrangements

Our efforts to promote and maintain collective self-defense arrangements begin with NATO. NATO has been the bedrock of Western security for nearly half a century. It is NATO that has enabled the Allies to win the Cold War; it is NATO that will remain the keystone of European security for the long term.

Today, changes in and around Europe pose new security problems that require a renewed Atlantic Alliance.

The role of security assistance here is clear. In order for several of our allies to have the confidence and capability to make a full contribution to the Alliance, they need our help. Their contributions to Desert Storm demonstrate the wisdom of our policies. I will outline our proposal for aid to NATO and other security partners later in my testimony.

Reduce Threats to Our Security and That of Others

Proliferation is a global problem that the Administration has been attacking on a global basis; indeed, in just a few days, I am making a trip to China that will focus on advancing our non-proliferation objectives. I hope soon to travel to South Asia to advance those same objectives. The Presidential initiative announced May 13, 1990 under which we have proposed to destroy our entire stock of chemical weapons, has set the stage

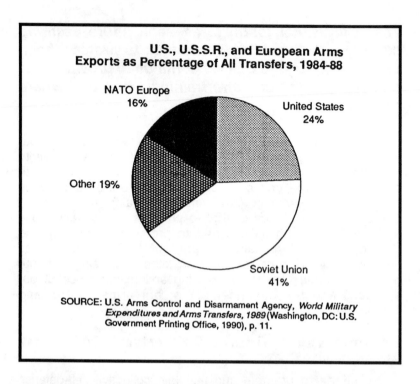

U.S., U.S.S.R., and European Arms Exports as Percentage of All Transfers, 1984-88

NATO Europe 16%

United States 24%

Other 19%

Soviet Union 41%

SOURCE: U.S. Arms Control and Disarmament Agency, *World Military Expenditures and Arms Transfers, 1989* (Washington, DC: U.S. Government Printing Office, 1990), p. 11.

for achieving a global treaty banning chemical weapons within a year. In the Australia Group, U.S. leadership has produced a breakthrough in worldwide control of exports of chemical weapons and precursors and chemical weapons-related dual-use equipment. And in missile non-proliferation, U.S. activism in the recent past has promoted the expansion of the Missile Technology Control Regime (MTCR) from seven to sixteen countries.

Help Our Friends Defend Themselves Against Threats

As we seek to persuade friends to take difficult steps toward non-proliferation and arms control, we must ensure that they can defend themselves against threats, both internal and external.

There are a number of different threats with which our friends may be concerned, and those threats vary on a regional basis. Addressing those threats calls for different discriminate responses.

For many, the threat is the familiar one: state-to-state violence, brought on by any one of the number of factors that can lead to war.

Some of our friends face purely internal threats, brought on

```
┌─────────────────────────────────────────────────────────────────┐
│                                                                   │
│   TOP TEN WEAPONS EXPORTERS AND IMPORTERS, 1990*                  │
│                                                                   │
│      Top Ten Suppliers          Top Ten Recipients               │
│                                                                   │
│       1. United States           1. Saudi Arabia                 │
│       2. Soviet Union            2. Japan                        │
│       3. France                  3. India                        │
│       4. United Kingdom          4. Afghanistan                  │
│       5. West Germany            5. Spain                        │
│       6. China                   6. Turkey                       │
│       7. Czechoslovakia          7. Greece                       │
│       8. Netherlands             8. North Korea                  │
│       9. Sweden                  9. Angola                       │
│      10. Italy                  10. Czechoslovakia              │
│       * Major conventional weapons                               │
│                                                                   │
│   Sources: SIPRI, CDI                                            │
│                                                                   │
│   Table prepared by Center for Defense Information               │
│                                                                   │
└─────────────────────────────────────────────────────────────────┘
```

by political and economic inequalities that have persisted over time, economic mismanagement, subversion, or natural disaster. Here our response is clear: we must promote and consolidate democratic values, promote free market principles, encourage full respect for human rights, and meet urgent humanitarian needs.

Other friends face new, transnational threats—drug trafficking and environmental degradation in particular. These threats, too, must be met in the most appropriate fashion.

Indeed, some of our friends even face anachronistic Marxist revolutions, led by those who have not yet recognized the ideological bankruptcy of communism.

Where these threats can be met adequately with economic assistance, that is our clear preference. But in many cases they cannot. The reality is that, for the foreseeable future, assuring stability—and enabling our friends to protect themselves—will require that we continue to provide arms and related services and training when and where appropriate.

It is this logic that underlines the Administration's position on arms sales in the President's proposal on arms control in the

Middle East. What we hope to prevent is one country's arming itself beyond legitimate self-defense needs and creating destabilizing military balances in a volatile region. Previously, there has been no multilateral system to monitor these types of build-ups. There were no international guidelines. No agreement exists among the nations that provide weapons to the region to allow transfers to be challenged as destabilizing.

What we propose to do now is what politics—"the art of the possible"—permits. We do not seek a regime that halts arms transfers, but we have proposed one that will seek to ensure that sales that do take place are responsible.

One of my principal messages today is that—while we are responding to the changes in the world around us—the security assistance "system" isn't broken. Rather, the system of international security relationships that we have forged over time is fundamentally sound and supportive of vital U.S. interests, as Desert Storm clearly demonstrates. We need now to build on this success. Let me talk about our regional programs to show you why this is the case.

Near East and South Asia ($5.51 Billion)

The success of our international security relationships—as well as the continuing needs—are especially evident in the Near East and South Asia regions.

In the Gulf War, Israel pursued a policy of restraint based on strength—military strength, and the strength derived from strong U.S.-Israeli security relations. We remain unshakably committed to Israel's security—a commitment that we demonstrated with the deployment of U.S. Patriot missile systems and U.S. crews in the Persian Gulf War. We are also committed to ensuring that Israel maintains its qualitative edge, built upon superiority in advanced weapons, as well as in command, control, communications and intelligence systems.

We are requesting security assistance for several other friends in the region whose help was critical to the success of Desert Storm—and whom we expect to be positive forces for stability in the post-crisis environment.

Europe ($1.21 billion)

The Gulf crisis again underscored the long-term, strategic importance of Turkey in two theaters—Europe and the Middle East. Throughout the crisis, Turkey was vital to the success of coalition efforts. Turkey was among the first to take concrete—and costly—actions to enforce sanctions against Iraq. Its shutting down of Iraq's oil pipeline was as important to the isolation of Iraq as the naval blockade. The presence of Turkey's armed forces, deployed along its border with Iraq, effectively pinned down ten Iraqi divisions. Turkey provided key bases from which U.S. forces were able to carry out attacks on Iraqi military facilities. These and other supportive Turkish actions saved many American lives.

Our security assistance effort ($625 million) is designed to assist the Turks in continuing the multi-year program to modernize their air defense forces.

Programs in Greece ($350 million) and Portugal ($165 million) are important as well. We have a continuing interest in assisting Greece with the modernization of its military to support fulfillment of its NATO roles. Greece is a democratic state which can serve as a force for stability in the Balkans. Our program in Portugal supports that country's multi-year force modernization effort which focuses on air/sea defense of the North Atlantic sea lanes and on access to the Mediterranean Sea.

American Republics ($980 million)

There are two major elements in our security assistance programs in the American Republics: support for the President's Andean counter-narcotics strategy, and support for peace and economic development in Central America.

As President Bush said in his State of the Union address, the war on drugs remains a national priority. To that end, in addition to a request for $171.5 million for the Bureau of International Narcotics Matters, we are requesting $412 million for Colombia, Bolivia, and Peru to help these democracies confront narcotics trafficking and develop their fragile economies.

In Central America, much of our effort remains focused on war-torn El Salvador ($120 million). Our assistance remains critical to the development of a comprehensive economic program to reform interest rates, narrow fiscal deficits, provide incentives for investment, and provide balance-of-payment support—just as it is in Nicaragua, Honduras, Guatemala, and Costa Rica.

These assistance programs complement the President's Enterprise for the Americas Initiative (EAI), and its key trade, investment, and debt proposals.

Africa ($52 million)

In Africa, our security assistance is requested for countries that have been our close partners and for support of new movement toward democracy. For the Development Fund for Africa, our principal vehicle for overall assistance, we seek an additional $800 million to promote broad and sustainable economic growth. We also seek to expand our regional approach to military assistance to enable timely assistance in resolving Africa's devastating internal conflicts.

East Asia and Pacific ($343 million)

Our clear emphasis in the East Asia and Pacific region is the Philippines ($320 million). A stable, democratic and prosperous Philippines with friendly ties to, and continued close security cooperation with, the United States is essential to the peace and stability of Southeast Asia, as well as to broad U.S. strategic interests in Asia. Here again, our access provided important support for Desert Shield and Desert Storm.

We are faced with a number of difficult—but not impossible—challenges as we attempt to ensure security and stability abroad. Our international cooperation programs will play an important part in our efforts. We believe that we have a very good package in place, and that the Administration's programs and requests make the proper adaptations for a changing world.

12   CURBING WORLD ARMS SALES

MAKING IT EASIER TO BUY ARMS

Gary Milhollin

Gary Milhollin is a professor at the University of Wisconsin Law School and serves as director of the Wisconsin Project on Nuclear Arms Control. This reading was excerpted from an article by Milhollin which originally appeared in the Washington Post, July 22, 1990.

Points to Consider:

1. How has a 1990 change in U.S. arms export law made it easier for the Third World to buy atomic weapons?

2. What factors make this decontrol a "shoppers paradise" for nations such as Pakistan, Iran and Libya?

3. Why were certain items decontrolled in the first place?

4. Describe the options for curbing this global arms race as outlined by the author.

Gary Milhollin, "Attention, Nuke-Mart Shoppers!", **The Washington Post,** July 22, 1990.

In the 1990s, the East-West arms race is being replaced by a North-South arms race.

In its haste to end the Cold War, the West is making it easier for the Third World to get the bomb.

On July 1, 1990, the United States and its allies lifted export controls on the very nuclear weapon triggers, called krytons, that Iraq tried to smuggle out of the United States in March. Now nations can buy these triggers over-the-counter in Eastern Europe. So can Pakistan, India, Israel, South Africa and any other country trying to make nuclear weapons.

Also decontrolled were "skull furnaces", which Iraq had been trying to get from a company in New Jersey. The furnaces can melt plutonium for nuclear bomb cores and melt titanium for missile nose cones. They are now on a dock in the Delaware River, blocked by the Pentagon on the last legal ground possible: that the exporter "knows or has reason to know" that they will be used in "fabricating. . .nuclear weapons." This remarkable stand is the first U.S. declaration that Iraq has an active A-bomb effort.

The move to decontrol was made by COCOM, the Coordinating Committee on Multilateral Export Controls, composed of Australia, Japan and all the NATO countries except Iceland. The intent was to help Eastern Europe develop its economy. But the effect will also be to help other countries build nuclear arms.

Through what was apparently an amazing oversight, the Bush administration agreed in a COCOM meeting in June to decontrol 30 categories of strategic equipment—most of which are on the dream list of Third World bomb makers. In the words of one U.S. export official: "This is a big problem the administration missed—they were warned about it but they didn't listen."

COCOM also decontrolled spin forming machines (which U.S. officials earlier tried to stop Iraq from getting from Germany) used to make uranium gas centrifuges, as well as vacuum pumps. With fewer than a thousand centrifuges, Iraq can produce enough weapons-grade uranium for one Hiroshima-size bomb per year. With vacuum pumps, Iraq can move fragile uranium gas through the centrifuges. Only last year, U.S. officials seized vacuum pumps that Iraq was trying to import from the United States without a license.

These problems are just the beginning. Want some "maraging steel?" In 1987, a Pakistani was arrested in

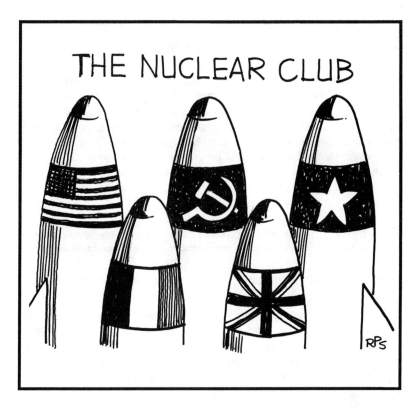

THE NUCLEAR CLUB

Philadelphia for trying to smuggle this special alloy, particularly suited for making centrifuges, out of the United States. Now, anybody can buy it by the ton. How about a plasma torch, or a high-speed oscilloscope? Plasma torches can nickel-plate the surface of a plutonium metal bomb core, such as the one that destroyed Nagasaki. Plating makes the core safe to handle. High-speed oscilloscopes can process the rapid data from nuclear tests. They can also help develop missile guidance systems, and can receive and sort the data from missile flight tests. Now both will go to the highest bidder.

Decontrolling Arms Exports

Several factors make this decontrol a bonanza for neophyte bomb makers. First, when an item is dropped from the COCOM list, it can be sold to buyers in Eastern Europe without a license. Nuclear triggers can go to Romania, Hungary or Czechoslovakia like bags of onions. There will be no shipment records and no limits on re-export. This means that other nations can order U.S. A-bomb triggers (and oscilloscopes) through Eastern Europe without breaking any laws. Iraq and Libya have already used European front companies to import chemical weapon plants.

Even if there were some strings attached to sales to Eastern Europe (such as a pledge not to re-export an item without permission) there would still be a great risk of diversion. These cash-starved regimes do not have functioning export control systems. Until they do, their companies can break the conditions of sale at minimal risk.

COCOM made these changes because German exporters, celebrating the end of the Cold War, demanded cuts in the control list. Faced with this demand, the Joint Chiefs of Staff produced a study that selected the few technologies the Pentagon thought it needed to stay ahead of the Soviets—"stealth" airplanes being an example. The Chiefs then agreed to decontrol the rest. For the Chiefs, it was more important to fight the Cold War than to stop the spread of the bomb. As usual, the generals were thinking of the last war.

What makes these changes so important is that they are happening at the very moment when the Third World is rushing to build weapons of mass destruction. In the Middle East, Iran, Iraq and Libya have all imported chemical weapons plants. They are now trying to import nuclear weapons and long-range missiles. In South Asia, India and Pakistan are threatening to have the world's first nuclear-armed border war—made possible by nuclear imports. In South America, Argentina and Brazil are teetering on the nuclear brink. And elsewhere, Israel and South Africa, pursuing their unique alliance, are building and testing long-range missiles together. In the 1990s, the East-West arms race is being replaced by a North-South arms race. Our export policies have not caught up with that fact.

Best Solution Impossible

What can be done? "The best solution," said one U.S. official, "would be to back up and do it right the first time." By that he meant that we should not have thrown out East-West controls before making sure that North-South controls stayed in place. Although legislation might help, neither of the two export bills pending in Congress recognizes the problem. According to a Senate staffer, the House bill, which loosens controls even more, "might as well be called the Proliferation Facilitation Act."

In our haste, we have made the best solution impossible. Now, we can only try to back-fit controls before too much bomb and missile technology rushes from the North to the South.

U.S. law, which still controls several items dropped off the COCOM list, shows how that might be done. Because of U.S. policy against nuclear and missile proliferation, the U.S. goods that can now go to Eastern Europe still cannot be exported directly to Third World bomb makers. For our NATO partners to adopt similar rules, they would have to declare frankly that they oppose the spread of nuclear bombs and missiles—and be ready to take the heat from the Third World. No longer could they blame COCOM for standing between them and their customers. So far, it is not clear that they will do that. If they don't, their companies will start selling the means to make the bomb, regardless of what the United States does.

But even if our NATO allies cooperate, we will need the cooperation of the old East Bloc. It will do no good to stop sales from Western Europe if Iraq and Libya can fill their orders through Eastern Europe. Bringing in the East Bloc would also put a fence around the technology that Eastern Europe is developing on its own. What we need is an anti-proliferation fence around both Eastern and Western Europe.

There are three ways to build it: use the Nuclear Non-Proliferation Treaty, use the European Community, or use a new version of COCOM. The treaty probably won't work. Although its members have already agreed to control a list of exports, the treaty's peculiar language limits the list to plutonium and enriched uranium, the two fission bomb fuels, and the equipment directly needed to make them. The list does not cover the hundred or so other commodities, such as nuclear weapon triggers, that are used to make or test nuclear bombs but do not produce bomb fuel. Such commodities are known as "dual-use items"—they also have civilian applications. Treaty members have consistently refused to expand the treaty's list to cover these items.

The European Community probably won't work either. Although it already contains the NATO countries, and may soon bring in Eastern Europe, it is still in the formative stages, has many other issues to face and has little competence in export control. Furthermore, the United States has no official access to EC deliberations.

The best choice for controlling nuclear commodities is a new COCOM—with a new mission aimed at nuclear and missile non-proliferation instead of the East-West arms race. To make such a group work, the East Bloc would have to join.

But would it? Eastern Europe obviously won't join in order to obtain the technology that COCOM has already decontrolled. Now, the West must offer a different incentive. One such incentive is economic aid. Export controls would be a small price to pay for such a boost.

The second carrot in Western hands is the technology that COCOM still controls. COCOM could gradually exchange this technology for cooperation on North-South issues. This would appeal to the Soviet Union, which wants the technology and has its own special concerns about nuclear proliferation. There is no reason why the entire East Bloc could not become part of a new group (with a new name) that included COCOM and operated in the same informal way as COCOM does.

The new group would have two goals: keeping nuclear bombs and missiles out of the Third World, and promoting trade among its members. Trade would increase along with non-proliferation controls. Organizing this would take some work, and there would still be a transition period during which NATO members of the new group denied technology to Eastern Europe. The result, however, would be much better than spreading the bomb to the Third World.

13   CURBING WORLD ARMS SALES

PREVENTING WEAPONS PROLIFERATION

Richard A. Clarke

Richard A. Clarke is the Assistant Secretary for Politico-Military Affairs, U.S. Dept. of State.

Points to Consider:

1. How are weapons of mass destruction defined?

2. What nations have weapons of mass destruction?

3. How are multi-national efforts helping to curb the arms trade?

4. What positive steps has the Bush Administration taken to slow missile proliferation?

5. How does the author agree that nuclear weapons and technology sales have been slowed?

Excerpted from testimony by Richard A. Clarke before the House Committee on Foreign Affairs, July 11, 1990.

We shall continue to work with other concerned nations to assure that technological progress does not translate into a greater risk of nuclear weapons spread.

Today, some fourteen countries possess a ballistic missile capability, including three with indigenously produced systems, and this number is growing. About twenty countries are pursuing offensive chemical weapons programs. About ten countries have biological weapons programs. In addition to the declared nuclear weapon states, there are a few Non-Proliferation Treaty (NPT) parties that have the capacity to rapidly deploy nuclear weapons.

The Bush administration has recognized the urgency of the situation and has determined to take every appropriate action to prevent, slow and deter the further spread of weapons of mass destruction. We created last year a high level Policy Coordinating Committee to bring together the strands of our large interagency community and improve communication and coordination on this issue. Recognizing that the threat is virtually global, involving countries and regions of varying political and economic importance, we realized early on that there are no simple, easy solutions. We decided to build upon past efforts, to make them more effective, and to devise new and imaginative strategies. We also realized that unilateral action by the U.S. alone would not be very effective, and have sought to fashion multilateral programs that would involve all states willing to cooperate with us.

Serious Concerns and Positive Steps

Although the Iraqis have taken center stage, almost every country in the Middle East has some missile capability. Many of them are seeking to buy new missiles or to obtain foreign help in developing their own. One of the most disturbing reports was that China was preparing to sell M-9 missiles to Syria. As you know, the Chinese have publicly stated that they have no plans to do so. We were pleased with the Chinese statement, but we continue to press China for more specific assurances on other countries, other missiles, and missile technology.

In Asia, a disturbing development has been the emergence of North Korea as a missile supplier. The North Koreans appear willing to sell Scud-based missiles to anyone who can pay for them.

The F-5 fighter has been exported to 32 foreign nations and has been manufactured in South Korea, Taiwan, and Switzerland.

In South Asia, the efforts of both India and Pakistan to develop missiles remain disturbing. The Indian program is more advanced, having fired the medium range Agni missile once and the short range Prithvi twice. We have had extensive discussions to discourage both sides from continuing to develop missiles—a potentially destabilizing weapons systems— in the region.

In other parts of the world, missile developments are less immediately threatening. In Latin America, for example, our main concern is that missiles developed there might be sold to the Middle East.

The Bush Administration views these developments with serious concern and has taken positive steps to slow missile proliferation. The U.S. has strengthened its internal procedures to review export cases involving missile technology. Since the first of this year, the interagency groups which were created—the MTEC (Missile Technology Export Control Group) and MTAG (Missile Trade Analysis Group)—have been reviewing about 140 cases per month, about 130 from State's Office of Defense Trade Controls (DTC) and 10 from Commerce.

In addition we have worked closely with the Intelligence Community to identify missile procurement efforts in other

```
┌─────────────────────────────────────────────────────┐
│                                                       │
│              RECOGNIZING THE URGENCY                   │
│                                                       │
│     The Bush administration has recognized the        │
│  urgency of the situation and has determined to take   │
│  every appropriate action to prevent, slow and deter   │
│  the further spread of weapons of mass destruction.    │
│                                                       │
│  U.S. Department of State, July, 1990                  │
│                                                       │
└─────────────────────────────────────────────────────┘
```

supplier countries.

We attended an Missile Technology Control Regime (MTCR) multilateral meeting in London last December. At that meeting, the partners agreed on the importance of securing wider adherence to and observance of the Guidelines. It is important to bring in all other European Commission (EC) countries before 1992, and we appear to making progress toward that goal.

We have had a number of meetings with the Soviets on missile proliferation issues, some in the context of periodic bilateral meetings of experts, others under the umbrella of Baker-Shevardnadze ministerials. The Soviets appear to be serious about controlling missile proliferation, and since they have been major suppliers of Scuds and other missiles to many countries over the years, this is an important development. These talks contributed to a joint statement issued at the recent Summit, in which both sides, among other things:

—affirmed their support for the objectives of the MTCR and called on all nations which have not done so to observe the spirit and guidelines of the regime,

—stated that they are restricting missile proliferation on a worldwide basis,

—agreed to work to stop missile proliferation, particularly in regions such as the Middle East, affirming their intent to explore regional initiatives.

It is significant that we and the Soviets could agree on a summit joint statement on missile proliferation, a relatively new element in our bilateral dialogue. We are further encouraged by the Soviets stated willingness to observe the guidelines of the MTCR.

Deputy Assistant Secretary for nonproliferation affairs, Elizabeth Verville, recently completed a trip through Eastern Europe to bring the nonproliferation issue to the attention of the new governments there. In Hungary, Yugoslavia, Romania, Poland, and Czechoslovakia, she met with a uniformly favorable reception. All of the governments stated that they shared our concerns about proliferation, and all indicated a desire to control it.

Efforts to Curb Proliferation

The proliferation of chemical and biological weapons, particularly in the Middle East, continues. As CIA Director Webster has noted in previous testimony, about 20 countries may be developing chemical weapons and approximately 10 have BW (biological weapons) programs.

The threat is grave. What are we doing about it?

The best long-term solution to the production, stockpiling, and use of CW (chemical weapons) is the conclusion of an effective global ban. We are working hard at the Conference on Disarmament in Geneva to create a treaty text that will address the complex issues involved in a total ban of CW.

While we are striving to achieve a global ban, we have been working on many fronts to prevent, slow, and deter chemical weapons proliferation.

Recognizing that we and the Soviet Union are the major possessors of chemical weapons stockpiles, we have held frequent talks with the Soviet Union on nonproliferation efforts.

We intend to continue our bilateral cooperation with the Soviet Union both in supporting the Geneva negotiations and in the nonproliferation area. More expert-level talks with the Soviets are planned.

In addition to the major multilateral task of achieving a treaty at Geneva, our primary mechanism for stemming the proliferation of chemical weapons is the Australia Group, an informal organization of twenty industrialized countries (EC countries plus the U.S., Norway, Japan, Australia, New Zealand, Canada, Austria, and Switzerland). It meets a twice a year in Paris to exchange information on actual cases of proliferation concern and to coordinate export controls.

Beyond the Australia Group members, there are a number of other countries that have sophisticated chemical industries and would be capable of supplying precursors. We have made overtures to these countries explaining how the U.S. and other Australia Group members control exports and have urged them to adopt similar controls.

The U.S. currently controls nine chemical precursors on a

worldwide basis, and an additional forty-one are controlled by Syria, Libya, Iraq and Iran. Of course actual chemical weapons themselves are strictly controlled under the Arms Export Control Act. We do not export chemical weapons.

Currently we are reviewing our export controls to determine how to expand their effectiveness. While I cannot go into the details of the discussions, I can say that we are seriously examining the feasibility of controlling the export of additional items which can contribute to CW.

The best long-term solution to problems of CW proliferation and use are multilateral in nature. We should ensure that our domestic legislation and policies contribute to rather than detract from that objective.

Progress on Biological Weapons

Biological weapons differ from CW in that there is already a treaty in existence which outlaws them. The U.S. destroyed its BW a long time ago. However, the unfortunate fact is that a number of countries are in violation of the Biological Weapons Convention (BWC) of 1972. We have detailed these countries in classified hearings.

All BW agents and most organisms capable of assisting in the production of BW require export licenses to any destination. However, the problem in BW is that the quantities needed are so small in comparison to CW precursors or agents that control is extremely difficult. One can literally carry enough BW seed stock in a pocket to enable a would-be proliferator to reproduce militarily significant amounts in a short time.

U.S. Supports International Efforts

The non-proliferation effort of longest standing has been aimed at preventing the spread of nuclear weapons to additional countries. Our concern about preventing nuclear proliferation goes back to the very dawn of the nuclear age, and over the years it has placed heavy demands on our resources and ingenuity. The results of our efforts can be seen today in a highly developed international system of nuclear non-proliferation instruments, institutions and controls.

Foremost among the legal instruments that underpin this system is the Treaty on the Non-Proliferation of Nuclear Weapons (NPT) with 140 parties, and for which we continue to seek universal participation. Supplementing and complementing it is the Treaty for the Prohibition of Nuclear Weapons in Latin

America (Treaty of Tlatelolco), which provides the basis for a nuclear weapons free zone in the region.

The central institutional structure is the International Atomic Energy Agency (IAEA), which implements a vital system of safeguards, making possible international cooperation in the peaceful uses of nuclear energy. The major nuclear supplier countries have agreed to abide by stringent export norms set forth in the Nuclear Supplier Group Guidelines and the NPT Exporter's Committee (Zangger Committee) Guidelines.

Contrary to the fears of many in the early days of the atom bomb, this system has worked, and it has worked well. Non-proliferation is inherently a process aimed at negation. Progress is measured, therefore, by what has not happened. And what has not happened, clearly, is an inexorable spread of nuclear weapons across the globe. Rather, there are today, as there have been for more than 25 years, only five acknowledged Nuclear Weapon States. Two of them—the U.S. and USSR—are currently deeply engaged in a major effort to reduce their nuclear arsenals.

The international nuclear non-proliferation regime stands as an example of the challenges that must be faced in assuring against the misuse of an advanced technology.

The system is in place, and it has proven itself effective. Our challenge, in some ways more difficult, is to protect, and where necessary, enhance the existing system to ensure that it will continue to function as one of the primary guarantors of U.S. national security and indeed of security for all nations.

14   CURBING WORLD ARMS SALES

STOPPING THE ARMS MERCHANTS

James Raffel and Gregory A. Bischak

James Raffel is a research analyst and Gregory A. Bischak is the Executive Director of the National Commission for Economic Conversion and Disarmament (ECD) located at 1801 Eighteenth Street, N.W., Washington, D.C. The Commission's major publication is The New Economy *from which the following article was excerpted.*

Points to Consider:

1. Who are the arms merchants?

2. What is the purpose behind the arms policy of the United States?

3. How can global arms sales be stopped?

4. What is the relationship of arms exports and the domestic economy?

5. How is economic conversion defined?

James Raffel and Gregory A. Bischak, "Stopping the Arms Merchants," **The New Economy,** April-May, 1991.

Peace and disarmament activists must advance alternatives to militarism in order to counter the economic and political forces that propel arms exports.

Before the smoke has cleared from our war with Iraq, the Bush Administration has proposed increasing arms sales to the Middle East, thus ignoring the horrible lesson of how sophisticated weapons produce instability and conflict. Indeed, the administration's intentions are reflected in its controversial proposal to amend the charter of the Export-Import Bank to provide financing for nations wishing to purchase weapons directly from U.S. arms manufacturers. The Pentagon, for its part, is using the prospect of massive arms sales abroad to keep military factories open, thus attempting to maintain the nation's military-industrial base and postpone indefinitely conversion to civilian production.

At first glance, the Bush Administration's efforts to stop the proliferation of weapons of mass destruction and dual-use technology stands in sharp contrast to its eagerness to sell more conventional arms abroad. From the administration's standpoint, however, the issues are as different as apples and oranges. Although the Cold War is over, Washington's goal of maintaining global military superiority and keeping potential rivals divided against each other remains unchanged. By selling conventional arms and aircraft abroad while maintaining tight controls over weapons of mass destruction, the United States is attempting to maintain its hegemony over the developing world and preserve its military-industrial base.

Arms Sales

Calls for a temporary ban on weapons sales to the Middle East may make sense as a way to focus Congressional and public attention on the need for controls on arms exports. But we must not lose sight of the larger goal: the demilitarization of foreign affairs and international trade. It is equally important that we not allow the Administration to bury disarmament by promoting arms exports.

Two proposals merit close consideration as ways to reverse the political and economic forces propelling arms sales: the creation of an international inspectorate to monitor and enforce bans on arms transfers; and the political commitment by the nations of the North and the South to convert arms industries to civilian use. The creation of a truly international inspectorate to regulate and control the trade in conventional weapons and

Sales of 12 Largest Western European and U.S. Defense Firms, 1988

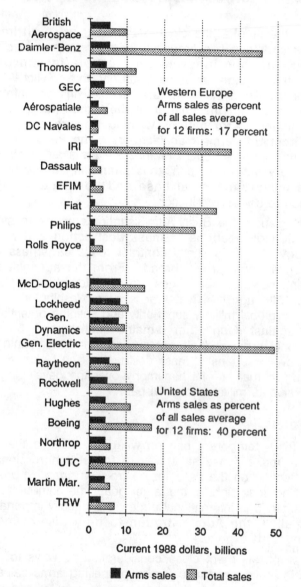

Western Europe
Arms sales as percent
of all sales average
for 12 firms: 17 percent

United States
Arms sales as percent
of all sales average
for 12 firms: 40 percent

Current 1988 dollars, billions

■ Arms sales   ▨ Total sales

SOURCE: Office of Technology Assessment, from data in Stockholm
International Peace Research Institute, SIPRI Yearbook 1990,
World Armaments and Disarmament (Oxford: Oxford University
Press, 1990), pp. 326-328.

dual-use technologies must be done through democratic international institutions. An inspectorate would enable the developing world to retain access to the goods and services it needs to create competitive national economies, while building important new institutions for conflict resolution. Efforts to stop the proliferation of weapons of mass destruction are doomed to fail, however, if the North continues to insist on using international institutions to enhance its security at the expense of the South. Meanwhile, all nations could benefit from transferring their economic resources from military production to vital civilian applications (the term for this process is called economic conversion). Yet it is clear that the search for political advantage and short-run profits fuel the worldwide arms trade, as they have for more than two decades.

Arms and Influence

Arms sales first became a staple of U.S. foreign policy toward the end of the Vietnam war. In response to Washington's disastrous involvement in that conflict, President Nixon outlined the "Nixon Doctrine" in 1969. The doctrine, in effect, announced that the United States would no longer intervene directly to protect its interests abroad, but would rely on regional clients to do so. This doctrine was applied soon afterward to the closest American ally in the Middle East, the Shah of Iran, who was permitted to buy the most sophisticated non-nuclear weapons in the U.S. arsenal. The policy suffered a serious setback in 1979, however, when the Shah was overthrown. Thus, when the Iran-Iraq war began in 1981, Washington found a new regional client in Saddam Hussein, whose military power was sought to checkmate Iran.

During the Iran-Iraq war, the United States encouraged other nations to sell weapons to Baghdad, because it feared that an Iranian victory would promote the spread of Islamic fundamentalism throughout the region. As a result of this obsession with establishing a regional balance of power which favored American interests, Iraq became one of the world's leading arms importers in the 1980s. The United States, for its part, sold Baghdad $1.5 billion worth of dual-use technologies from 1985 to 1990.

These arms and technology transfers to Baghdad, however, only succeeded in inspiring militarization and instability in the region, culminating in the invasion of Kuwait. The failure of this arms transfer policy to bring about a stable balance of power in the region underscores once again the inherent flaws of such a policy.

As a consequence of this failure, Washington began reviewing its non-proliferation policies. Last December, 1990, the Bush Administration unveiled its "Enhanced Proliferation Control Initiative," (EPCI), the public goal of which is to stop U.S. exports of technologies and materials which may be used to make chemical or biological weapons or missiles. The real goal of the policy, however, is to insure U.S. military superiority over potential regional rivals by denying them the capability to build weapons of mass destruction. It is not surprising that some of the nations to be affected by the EPCI (Israel and Saudi Arabia for example) are nonetheless among the best customers for U.S. conventional weapons. Selling more conventional weapons abroad will not undermine U.S. military superiority, and, in the Bush Administration's view, will help shore up the regional balance of power.

Arms Exports and the Domestic Economy

Arms sales accounted for only 4.4 percent of all U.S. exports in 1988, according to the U.S. Arms Control and Disarmament Agency (ACDA). But for several of the largest U.S. military-contractors, especially McDonnell-Douglas, Raytheon and Westinghouse, arms exports constitute a substantial share of their business.

The Pentagon is responding to declining defense budgets by promoting arms exports as a means of maintaining the nation's military-industrial base. For example, one reason the Army cited in its recent decision not to close the General Dynamics Detroit Arsenal Tank Plant was that the facility produces 15 tank modification kits monthly for Egypt. The Air Force appears to be pursuing a similar strategy. In an effort to preserve an industrial base for production of the Multirole Fighter (MF), the planned successor to the F-16, the Air Force is taking an "increasingly active role" in supporting efforts by General Dynamics to sell the plane abroad, according to *Defense News*. South Korea's recent decision to purchase 120 F-16s therefore represents a victory for the Air Force's industrial policy, but is a setback to those wishing to promote economic conversion and disarmament.

Peace and disarmament activists must advance alternatives to militarism in order to counter the economic and political forces that propel U.S. arms exports. To demilitarize international affairs, both the North and the South will have to pursue economic conversion. Moreover, the time has come to create a truly international inspectorate to verify bans on arms transfers and controls on dual-use technologies.

No nation in the Middle East will seriously consider entering into an arms-reduction accord if it feels vulnerable to attack. To reduce the risk of war in the region, the United States should lead an international effort to create a series of regional confidence-building measures. One important component of any effort to promote regional demilitarization would be a ban on importing weapons.

Such a ban could be verified by a United Nations organization, perhaps modeled after the International Atomic Energy Agency. If international institutions for conflict resolution are to be effective, however, they must be binding on both the North and the South, and they must be used preventively to avert conflict.

The United Nations has considered a series of proposals for stemming the arms trade that deserve renewed attention today. If U.N. members disclosed the full size of their military budgets and their arms exports and imports, it would become possible to monitor accurately the arms trade, a necessary precondition for restraining it. A more effective regime will have to overcome the obstacles of national sovereignty and private property to permit inspections of production facilities. Creation of such an inspection system will not be easy, however. The West European signatories to the Conventional Forces in Europe Treaty (CFE) opposed creating such an inspection regime.

The Arms Trade, Conversion and Foreign Debt

Powerful economic forces help sustain the arms trade. If this market is ever to be curtailed, economic incentives must be created to discourage weapons production. Internationally, several heavily indebted developing countries such as Brazil, Argentina, India and Egypt have developed arms industries, in part because they seek export earnings in a lucrative market. Eastern European countries also are looking to arms exports as a means to earn hard currency to pay off their onerous debt burdens.

Among these nations, conversion of military-industries in exchange for debt reduction agreements with western debt-holders is one promising proposal for curbing the economic incentives to produce arms exports. The basic idea is that the external public debts of arms-exporting nations which are held by Western countries could be reduced in return for each country's conversion of its military production to civilian use. For example, debt relief could be linked to a reimbursement-in-cash agreement, whereby the debtor country would deposit the savings from reduced investments in state-owned arms production into a development fund. Each payment would count as a corresponding reduction in external public debt. The rate of debt reduction would be based on a negotiated formula matching payments to the hard currency value of the debt. The savings on debt service could then be channeled back into facilities converting to relevant civilian production. The principal in the development fund could be used for a variety of purposes, either to promote other development projects, or to insure against default of the agreement.

Forgiving debt is not a new idea. In contemporary international affairs, however, writing off debt is generally done to "reward" developing countries for complying with the North's political agenda. Washington's recent decision to forgive Egypt's $6.7 billion in military-related debts as a *quid pro quo* for Cairo's active support of Operation Desert Storm is a case in point. A more constructive approach to debt reduction is illustrated by Costa Rica's experiment with a debt reduction for nature conservation agreement. This arrangement provides an important model for other nations to emulate and extend in socially constructive ways. However, before the developing world will accept these conversion proposals as serious, the northern industrialized powers must curb their own militaristic appetites.

The alternatives to militarism outlined here would promote international peace and economic growth. In contrast, the Bush Administration's approach to "national security" issues will inspire international conflict and economic decline. It is the failure of past policies and the dangers presented by current efforts that makes consideration of alternatives essential.

15   CURBING WORLD ARMS SALES

ARMS SALES CAN HELP PRESERVE PEACE

Reginald Bartholomew

Reginald Bartholomew made the following statement in his capacity as Undersecretary of State for Coordinating Security Assistance Programs in the Bush Administration.

Points to Consider:

1. Describe the President's arms control proposal for the Middle East.

2. How can arms sales stabilize the region?

3. What does stabilize mean?

4. How does the policy toward conventional arms sales in the Middle East differ from the policy toward nuclear proliferation in the region?

Excerpted from testimony by Reginald Bartholomew before the Senate Foreign Relations Committee, June 6, 1991.

We do not believe that arms sales are necessarily destabilizing.

The Middle East is the area of the world that combines the largest inventories of weapons (including weapons of mass destruction and missiles) with the greatest frequency of major wars over the last twenty years. It is a region wherein arms control is virtually unknown. We begin, with the President's initiative, a walk down a path untraveled before by the countries of the region.

The President's Proposal

The President's proposal was not designed in a vacuum. Its development began while Iraqi forces were still in Kuwait. It has benefited from ideas proposed by others. It has been the result of consultations with Allied states and with countries in the region. It is meant to be compatible with suggestions such as those made by Prime Minister Major and President Mitterand.

In designing the initiative, we had several criteria in mind. Two of those important criteria were that the proposal should be comprehensive and that it should be realistic.

- **Comprehensive**: A proposal which addressed only weapons of mass destruction and overlooked the threat of conventional arms build-ups would not work. Within the realm of weapons of mass destruction, a proposal that addressed only chemical weapons and not nuclear development would also fall short. The President's proposal is comprehensive.

- **Realistic**: An initiative coming now must not seek to impose a European solution on the Middle East. It must set out goals that nations in the region could now achieve. Thus, we see these proposals as reasonable first steps. Tougher steps, such as limits on the conventional inventories of nations and the achievement of a zone free of weapons of mass destruction, could come later.

Let me turn now to the main elements of our proposal:

First, conventional arms. We have proposed that the five major suppliers of conventional arms to the region meet to discuss the creation of a regime to address the problem of potentially destabilizing military build-ups in the region. We have had discussions with all of the other four countries involved and believe they will all attend. The French have agreed to host the conference. I will lead a senior American delegation.

113

Photo credit: U.S. Department of Defense

Licensed production of the F-4EJ, which resembles these U.S. Air Force F-4Gs, began in the early 1970s and was an important source of technical know-how for the developing Japanese military aerospace industry. Other U.S. license production arrangements for fighter aircraft in Japan include the F-104 Starfighter and the F-15J.

Our goal is to ameliorate the conditions that can lead to war in this volatile region. The U.S. wants to prevent arming beyond legitimate self-defense needs and creating destabilizing military imbalances in this volatile region. Previously, there has been no system to monitor these types of build-ups. There were no guidelines to be violated. No agreement exists among nations that provide weapons to the region to allow transfers to be challenged as destabilizing.

We seek to put in place what was missing: a forum for the major suppliers, a code of conduct, transparency, and an opportunity to discuss problems before they get out of control.

To implement this regime, the suppliers would commit to observe a general code of responsible arms transfers; to avoid destabilizing transfers; and to establish effective domestic export controls on arms or dual-use technology to be transferred.

The guidelines for suppliers will include a mechanism for consultation among suppliers, who would notify one another in advance of certain arms sales; meet regularly to consult on arms transfers; consult on an ad hoc basis if a supplier believed guidelines were not being observed; and provide one another

ARMS SALES AND SECURITY

I emphasize that the past arms transfer policies of the United States, our supply of arms to Israel and to moderate Arab nations, did not contribute in the slightest to Iraq's aggression. Indeed, it was the military weakness of the Gulf Arab states that encouraged Saddam to move against Kuwait.

In fact, without these American sales, and without security relations built over decades, the defense of Saudi Arabia and the liberation of Kuwait would have been much more difficult. In particular, U.S.-built air bases and other support facilities — which constituted over a quarter of our military sales to Saudi Arabia over the past four decades — were vital to our ability to deploy forces quickly.

Henry S. Rowen, Assistant Secretary of Defense for International Security Affairs, in testimony before the Senate Foreign Relations Committee, June 6, 1991

with an annual report on transfers.

The suppliers would also seek to establish the highest standards on export controls related to the technologies that can contribute to missiles and weapons of mass destruction.

I know that some would have us go further than this proposal. We might. . .if this proposed regime can be achieved. The truth is, however, that this proposal will be tough for many of the other suppliers to accept. Based upon our preliminary discussions with them, we know that they have problems with transparency and other aspects of the regime.

This proposal is aimed at preventing future destabilizing conventional imbalances and caches of weapons of mass destruction. It is not aimed at preventing peaceful nations from having the ability to defend themselves. It is not aimed at stopping the international transfer of arms.

We do not believe that arms sales are necessarily destabilizing. Quite the contrary, we believe that the arms sales policy of the United States has been and is today aimed at supporting our strategic objective in the region — stability.

In this respect, we face the continuing challenge of strengthening our security relationships with our friends in the region and working with them to create shared security arrangements. A crucial element of this long-range process is helping our friends meet their legitimate defense and security needs. We have permitted friendly states to defend themselves to the degree that they reasonably can, and this has meant fewer crises, in general, and far fewer in which American men and women have had to risk their lives.

We will not seek a regime that halts arms transfers, but we have proposed one that will seek to ensure that sales that do take place are responsible.

That is why it is in no way a contradiction for the United States to be simultaneously seeking an arms transfer regime with the other major suppliers and continuing to supply arms needed by peaceful states to defend themselves against aggressors. We will resume sending to the Congress over the next few weeks those defense-related and weapon system transfers which we believe are in the best interests of the United States, the recipient states, and the cause of peace and stability.

For us to do otherwise would have the most adverse consequences on our ability to achieve the sort of system of stability in the Middle East which we all seek.

Second, **on missiles,** we are proposing that states in the region destroy their surface-to-surface missiles. Missiles are the most destabilizing weapons. They tend to target innocent civilians. They have been used against five countries in the region in the last five years.

We would begin with a freeze on the acquisition, production, and testing of surface-to-surface missiles. We would be prepared to help negotiate and verify such a regime. Suppliers would also step up efforts to coordinate export licensing for equipment, technology and services that could be used to manufacture surface-to-surface missiles.

Third, **on nuclear weapons,** we call for a verifiable regime to insure that no production of nuclear weapon grade material is taking place in the region. It also reiterates our call on all states in the region that have not already done so to accede to the Nuclear Non-Proliferation Treaty. It renews our call to place all nuclear facilities in the region under International Atomic Energy Agency safeguards. It once again asks that suppliers sell only when full scope safeguards will be in place. Finally, it continues to support the eventual creation of a nuclear weapon-free zone in Middle East.

Fourth, **on chemical weapons,** the proposal builds on the

President's recent initiative to achieve early completion of the global Chemical Weapons Convention. It calls for all states in the region to commit to becoming original parties to the Convention. Given the history of possession and use of chemical weapons in the region, the initiative also calls for regional states to institute confidence-building measures now, including national and bilateral trial inspections of facilities such as chemical plants.

Fifth, **on biological weapons,** we follow the same approach as on chemical weapons — building on an existing global approach.

Proliferation is a global problem, and the administration has been attacking it on a global basis.

The Gulf War has heightened not only our concern, but the world's concern over the global impact of instability in the Middle East, and it highlighted the need to move forward expeditiously to address one of the major underlying problems of regional instability — arms proliferation.

16   CURBING WORLD ARMS SALES

ARMING A DANGEROUS WORLD

The Center for Defense Information

The Center for Defense Information (CDI) supports an effective defense and opposes excessive expenditures for weapons and policies that increase the danger of war. The following article was taken from their public affairs journal called The Defense Monitor.

Points to Consider

1. Why is the U.S. increasing its weapons exports?

2. How does the global arms trade influence world events?

3. What has been the main reason given for U.S. arms sales in the past?

4. Identify the dollar amounts involved in the global arms trade.

5. How should the U.S. change its policy on arms sales?

"We Arm the World," **The Defense Monitor,** Vol. XX, Number 4, 1991.

The U.S. has taken a firm stand against trade in illegal drugs, but when it comes to the export of weapons, which kill far more people than drugs, the U.S. adopts a business-as-usual attitude.

People often say the United States can no longer effectively compete in exports. At least in regard to one particular market, that is untrue. When it comes to exporting weapons the U.S. is once again number one. According to the most recent information, the value of U.S. weapons deliveries to the entire world in 1990 exceeded the value of Soviet exports, reversing the previous order.

Despite the fact that the Cold War is over and Soviet arms transfers are dropping, the U.S. is planning to increase its weapons exports. This policy is the result of pressures both from U.S. weapons manufacturers concerned about increasing profits and the Pentagon, which wants to maintain a huge arms industry to support the military in future wars.

The recent war against Iraq warns us that a likely cause of future conflicts is unrestrained trade in conventional weapons. The U.S. is a major contributor to this trade. As the famous cartoon character Pogo said, "We have met the enemy and he is us." Despite fears about the use of "weapons of mass destruction", wars waged to date have been fought almost exclusively with conventional weapons. Resources devoted to the design and production of such weapons still constitute a heavy drain on the budgets of most countries in the world.

Despite the example of Iraq, the U.S. and other countries continue to treat weapons as just another export, allowing military contractors to make huge profits. This *laissez faire* attitude is the reverse of government attitudes on some other important trade matters. For example, the U.S. has taken a firm stand against trade in illegal drugs but when it comes to the export of weapons, which kill far more people than drugs, the U.S. adopts a business-as-usual attitude.

This policy now is particularly absurd. The main reason the U.S. has been exporting weapons since World War II has been to contain communism. With the Soviet Union now an economic basketcase struggling to hold itself together, the Soviet model has long since lost its appeal for other nations. Its cooperation with the U.S. regarding Iraq showed that the Soviet Union is willing to be a constructive participant in a Middle East peace process and reduce weapons sales in the future.

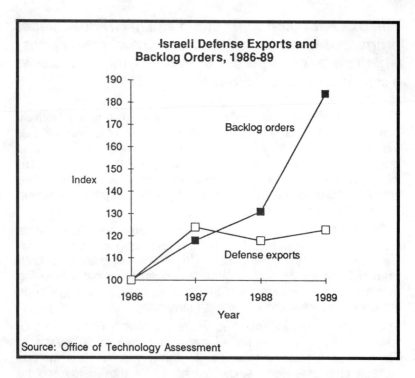

Israeli Defense Exports and Backlog Orders, 1986-89

Source: Office of Technology Assessment

Furthermore, with the defeat of Iraq, the Soviets lost one of their best customers.

Expanding Sales

Unfortunately, the U.S. continues to ignore the dangers of unrestrained arms sales. The U.S. is poised for a vast expansion of its overseas weapons sales. This is partly a reward to nations that helped the U.S. against Iraq and also an attempt to increase the business of U.S. military contractors who might otherwise have to shut down weapons plants.

According to preliminary estimates, over $41 billion worth of U.S. arms and military aid are to be sold or given to foreign countries in FY (fiscal year) 1991. Nearly $16 billion of this is projected to go to Middle East countries. This is a continuation of recent U.S. policies. A 1989 congressional report found that "military assistance which previously took 25-30 percent of the [foreign assistance] budget, increased to over 40 percent in the mid 1980s and has been running at 36 percent of the budget during the past three years."

This has a direct effect on the type of weaponry appearing on the world's battlefields. Wars are now more destructive due to the increased availability of advanced weapons facilitated by the spread of modern technology.

The immense destruction caused by unrestricted arms trade is of increasing concern. Senator John McCain (R-AZ) recently noted, "While the USSR dominated the arms trade during the last decade, six of the world's ten top merchants of death and mass destruction are Western democracies, and they accounted for $104 billion worth of arms sales out of the $261 billion sold by the top ten exporters over the last decade."

With regard to the sale and transfer of weapons, the old world order still dominates. The only difference is that the "merchant of death" is no longer a single individual. Instead he has been replaced by massive military industrial corporations and national security bureaucrats.

Too Many Arms

Since World War II there have been over 170 wars and conflicts, mostly involving countries which rely on foreign suppliers for their military needs. Thirty-one conflicts employing conventional weapons were fought around the globe in 1990.

In much of the developing world, military expenditures are almost four times the investment for health care and twice that for education. Military spending among the less developed countries in 1988 alone was $167.3 billion.

Since 1960 developing countries have increased military expenditures more than twice as fast as living standards. The 8-year conflict between Iran and Iraq alone is estimated to have employed some $60 billion worth of conventional weapons and caused, according to some estimates, over three million casualties.

Weapons transfers have been an integral element of regional mistrust and tension across the world. They continue to flow to nations from A to Z, including Afghanistan, where the U.S. has decided to ship 7,000 tons of captured Iraqi weapons for use by rebels fighting the Soviet-backed government, and Zaire, where the U.S. supports longtime dictator Mobuto Sese-Seko.

New U.S. Policies Should:

- Reduce all industrialized countries' weapons exports to the Third World. It is here that the bulk of the world conflicts are fought.

- Limit U.S. government weapons sales and government loans, grants, training, and construction for military purposes, as well as commercial sales by private firms.

- Establish specific limits, region by region. In regard to the Middle East, the U.S., along with the other permanent members of the U.N. Security Council, should seek a moratorium on new weapons transfers to the region. As a part of that process, regional stability must be improved by the implementation of confidence-building measures such as inspections and information exchanges.

- Make weapons sales more visible. Increasing the amount of information available about conventional weapons sales is one way to focus pressure against them. All nations should be required to submit the details of proposed weapons sales to the U.N. Military Staff Committee.

- Restrain arms sales within regions of extreme tension

before the outbreak of war.

- Base U.S. economic aid on the levels of military expenditures and arms imports of the recipient nation.

- Eliminate subsidies by U.S. taxpayers in the form of grants and "sweetheart" loans for arms transfers to Third World nations.

A recent report by the Office of Technology Assessment noted: "The threat of Soviet expansionism is greatly reduced, the possibility of a Warsaw Pact invasion of Western Europe has been eliminated, and the Soviet Union appears to be following a policy of restraint in arms exports. Accordingly, the defense requirements of the United States and its European allies are diminishing significantly. Moreover, a principal reason why the United States transferred weapons and defense technology to allied and friendly nations—to counter Communist influence—has been reduced."

If the United States is to lead the way to "a new world order under the rule of law," we must be the first to stem the flow of arms that fuel regional conflicts. The pursuit of profits must not be permitted to interfere with the creation of a more stable, peaceful community of nations.

RECOGNIZING AUTHOR'S POINT OF VIEW

This activity may be used as an individualized study guide for students in libraries and resource centers or as a discussion catalyst in small group and classroom discussions.

Many readers are unaware that written material usually expresses an opinion or bias. The capacity to recognize an author's point of view is an essential reading skill. The skill to read with insight and understanding involves the ability to detect different kinds of opinions or bias. *Sex bias, race bias, ethnocentric bias, political bias and religious bias* are five basic kinds of opinions expressed in editorials and all literature that attempts to persuade. They are briefly defined in the glossary below.

---

5 Kinds of Editorial Opinion or Bias

Sex Bias—the expression of dislike for and/or feeling of superiority over the opposite sex or a particular sexual minority

Race Bias—the expression of dislike for and/or feeling of superiority over a racial group

Ethnocentric Bias—the expression of a belief that one's own group, race, religion, culture or nation is superior. Ethnocentric persons judge others by their own standards and values.

Political Bias—the expression of political opinions and attitudes about domestic or foreign affairs

Religious Bias—the expression of a religious belief or attitude

---

Guidelines

1. Locate three examples of political opinion or bias in the readings from Chapter Four.

2. Locate five sentences that provide examples of any kind of editorial opinion or bias from the readings in Chapter Four.

3. Write down each of the above sentences and determine what kind of bias each sentence represents. Is it **sex bias, race bias, ethnocentric bias, political bias or religious bias**?

4. Make up one sentence statements that would be an example of each of the following: **sex bias, race bias, ethnocentric bias, political bias and religious bias.**

5. See if you can locate five sentences that are factual statements from the readings in Chapter Four.

Summarize author's point of view in one sentence for each of the following opinions:

Reading 10 _____

Reading 11 _____

Reading 12 _____

Reading 13 _____

Reading 14 _____

Reading 15 _____

Reading 16 _____

BIBLIOGRAPHY

Adams, James. Engines of War: Merchants of Death and the New Arms Race. New York: *Atlantic Monthly Press*, 1990: 307 p.

America's Arsenal. *Fortune*, v. 123, Feb. 25, 1991: p. 40-43.

Arms for Sale. *Newsweek*, v. 117, Apr. 8, 1991: p. 22-25.

Bani-Sadr. Stop Arming Dictators and Monarchs. *New Perspectives Quarterly*, v. 7, Fall 1990: p. 62-63.

Banks, H. Aerospace and Defense. *Forbes*, v. 145, Jan. 8, 1990: p. 122-3.

Banta, K.W. The Arms Merchant's Dilemma. *Time*, v. 135, Apr. 2, 1990: p. 29.

Brzoska, M. At Your Service: West German Trade. *The Bulletin of the Atomic Scientists,* v. 45, July/Aug. 1989: p. 34.

Brzoska, M. Behind the German Export Scandals. *The Bulletin of the Atomic Scientists,* v. 45, July/Aug. 1989: p. 32.

Budiansky, S. Back to the Arms Bazaar. *U.S. News and World Report*, v. 110, Apr. 1, 1991: p. 20-22.

Cardeon, C. Of Cluster Bombs and Kiwis—Children Arms to Iraq. *Time*, v. 136, Dec. 10, 1990: p. 71.

Cobb, J. and Zindar, J.M. Dealing Arms. *Common Cause Magazine,* v. 15, Mar./Apr. 1989: p. 23-27.

Cooper, J. Soviet Military Has a Finger in Every Pie. *The Bulletin of the Atomic Scientists,* v. 46, Dec. 1990: p. 22-25.

Flick, R. How We Appeased a Tyrant. *Reader's Digest,* v. 138, Jan. 1991: p. 39-44.

Fuhrman, P. It Couldn't Have Happened to a Nice Guy: French Arms Sales to Iraq. *Forbes,* v. 147, Mar. 4, 1991: p. 38-39.

Gandhi's Watergate? Indian Arms Scandal. *Newsweek,* v. 114, Oct. 23, 1989: p. 42.

Hammer, J. The German Connection. *Newsweek,* v. 117, Feb. 4, 1991: p. 57.

Hardt, John P. Guns into Butter, Soviet Style. *The Bulletin of the Atomic Scientists*, v. 46, Jan./Feb. 1990: p. 16-20.

Hornik, R. With a Little Help from Friends. *Time,* v. 135, June 11, 1990: p. 34.

Husbands, J. A Buyer's Market for Arms. *The Bulletin of the Atomic Scientists,* v. 46, May 1990: p. 14-16.

Klare, M.T. Fueling the Fire: How We Armed the Middle East. *The Bulletin of the Atomic Scientists,* v. 47, Jan./Feb. 1991: p. 18-26.

Klare, M.T. The American Arms Supermarket. *University of Texas Press,* 1984: 312 p.

Klare, M.T. The Arms Race Shifts to the Third World. *The Bulletin of the Atomic Scientists,* v. 46, May 1990: p. 2, 8-16.

Klare, M.T. Who's Arming Who? The Arms Trade in the 1990's. *Technology Review,* v. 93, May/June 1990: p. 42-50.

Letter from Europe—France's Arming of Iraq. *The New Yorker,* v. 67, Mar. 18, 1991: p. 85-91.

Lacayo, R. Choose Your Weapons. *Time,* v. 137, Mar. 18, 1991: p. 58.

Lief, L. Inside Bonn's Middle East Arms Bazaar. *U.S. News and World Report,* v. 108, May 28, 1990: p. 41.

Marshall, E. War with Iraq Spurs New Export Control. *Science,* v. 251, Feb. 1, 1991: p. 512-14.

Mecham, M. U.S. Suspends Military Sales in Wake of Massacre in China. *Aviation Week and Space Technology,* v. 130, June 12, 1989: p. 69-70.

Minard, L. and Fuhrman, P. No Trade-Ins: Soviet Loans Extended for Arms Purposes. *Forbes,* v. 147, Mar. 18, 1991: p. 42.

Morrocco, J.D. Pentagon Purchases Soviet Hardware on Open Market. *Aviation Week and Space Technology,* v. 130, Jan. 23, 1989: p. 24-25.

Negin, E. Fueling the Third World's Arms Race. *Scholastic Update,* v. 123, Mar. 22, 1991: p. 10.

Negin, E. Who Armed Saddam? *Scholastic Update,* v. 123, Mar. 22, 1991: p. 8-10.

Peacock, C. Arms Trade Flourishing Despite Cold War Thaw. *Utne Reader,* Nov./Dec. 1990: p. 35-36.

Phillips, A. Guns and Profits: The Gulf War May Spur Weapons Sales. *Maclean's,* v. 104, Apr. 1, 1991: p. 39.

Power, J. Arms and the Third World. *World Press Review,* v. 37, June 1990: p. 22.

Post, T. From Chile to Miami, Miami to Baghdad. *Newsweek,* v. 117, Apr. 8, 1991: p. 27-28.

Reverting to Form—Rearming the Middle East. *Commonweal,* v. 118, Apr. 5, 1991: p. 212-13.

Rinehart, D. From Nuclear Arms to Candy and Beer. *U.S. News and World Report,* v. 108, Feb. 19, 1990: p. 50-51.

Rossant, J. Adnan Khashoggi: He's Back. *Business Week,* Sept. 24, 1990: p. 45.

Schifrin, C.A. British Aerospace, General Dynamics Agree to Cooperate on Defense Projects. *Aviation Week and Space Technology,* v. 132, May 21, 1990: p. 26.

Schifrin, M. Shouldering Arms. *Forbes,* v. 143, Apr. 17, 1989: p. 208-9.

Schine, E. The Casualties of Peace. *Business Week,* Jan. 8, 1990: p. 70.

Smolowe, J. Who Armed Baghdad? *Time,* v. 137, Feb. 11, 1991: p. 34-35.

Thorpe, N. Swords into Plowshares. *World Press Review,* v. 38, Jan. 1991: p. 58.

The World's Most Dangerous Man. *U.S. News and World Report,* v. 108, June 4, 1990: p. 38-40.

Toy, S. Defense's Gravy Train Nears End of the Line. *Business Week,* Jan. 9, 1989: p. 75.

Wall Street's Myopia. *Aviation Week and Space Technology,* v. 132, May 28, 1990: p. 9.

World Weapons Sales Top $1 Trillion, Paced by South Asia Market. *Aviation Week and Space Technology,* v. 131, Aug. 28, 1989: p. 34-36.